GWJ ARCHITEKTUR

De aedibus

Der italienische Architekt und Architekturtheoretiker Aldo Rossi verglich die Architektur mit den Wissenschaften. Wie diese schreite die Architektur voran, indem sie stetig auf bereits Erreichtes aufbaue und sich so weiterentwickele. Diesem wissenschaftlichen Aspekt dient diese Buchreihe. Seit 2000 dokumentiert sie die aktuelle Schweizer Architektur. Die Reihe wird in ihrer Kontinuität gleichsam zu einem Gedächtnis der Architektur, das die Werke dem Vergessen entzieht. Von den mit hohem Qualitätsanspruch ausgewählten Architekturschaffenden werden die wichtigsten Bauten festgehalten, ausführlich dargestellt und dokumentiert. Jeder Band dient auch der Reflexion über den architektonischen Willen, der hinter den Projekten steht. So sind in dieser Reihe mehr oder minder alle in der Schweiz wirkenden Architekturkritikerinnen und Architekturkritiker mit einzelnen oder mehreren Textbeiträgen vertreten.

Der Hauptteil in jedem Band widmet sich dagegen der Welt der Anschauung. So sind jeweils anhand von Bildern und Plänen einige bemerkenswerte Bauten dargestellt, die nicht einer routinierten «Produktion» entsprungen sind. Vielmehr steht hinter jedem Entwurf eine leidenschaftliche Auseinandersetzung mit der Aufgabe und deren Prämissen.

Heinz Wirz
Verleger

De aedibus

The Italian architect and architectural theoretician Aldo Rossi compared architecture to the sciences. Like them, architecture progresses by constantly building upon what has already been achieved and develops further in this way. Since 2000, this series of books has been dedicated to the same academic approach in documenting contemporary Swiss architecture. It therefore becomes a form of architectural memory, ensuring that the architecture is not forgotten. The most important buildings by each of the selected high-quality architects are presented, described in detail and documented. Each volume also serves to reflect upon the architectural motivation behind the projects. By now, more or less every architectural critic working in Switzerland has contributed one or more articles to the series.

However, the core of each book is dedicated to the world of observation. Images and plans present a number of remarkable buildings that are not the result of routine "production". Instead, each design stems from a passionate engagement with the task and its premises.

Heinz Wirz
Publisher

117 De aedibus

GWJ ARCHITEKTUR

QUART

GWJ ÜBER 7 BEGRIFFE BEGREIFEN

Axel Simon

1. Bern

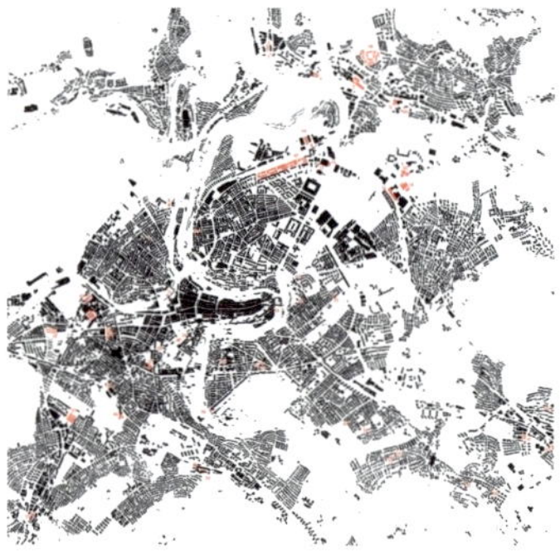

Ein unscheinbares Bürogebäude am Nordring in Bern, vielleicht hundertjährig. Das Architekturbüro GWJ belegt hier eine Etage – schon seit 25 Jahren, als der dortige Verlag seine Druckerei schloss. Tritt man aus dem Lift, steht man direkt im Büro. Der offene, beinahe leere Raum ist vom Glas der Besprechungsräume gefasst. In halbhohen Regalen stehen Modelle und Materialproben, Bücher und Magazine. Jenseits des Treppenhauskerns staunt man erst mal über eine riesige Pilzstütze, ein Erbe der ehemaligen Druckerei. Drum herum scharen sich die Tische der Mitarbeitenden; in Gruppen sitzen hier die Projektteams zusammen. Konzentrierte Betriebsamkeit und auffällige Diversität: viele Junge, verschiedene Nationalitäten. «Bravo, Selina!», gratuliert die Webseite des Büros zum Lehrabschluss und berichtet vom Sommerfest mit Pizza-Workshop.

GWJ ist jung, auch wenn es als Büro älter ist als viele seiner Mitarbeiterinnen und Mitarbeiter. Deren Altersdurchschnitt liegt bei 34 Jahren. «Wir werden nicht älter», sagen Nick Gartenmann, Donat Senn, Eva Herren und Christian Lasser, die von zwei Assoziierten bei der Führung unterstützt werden. Seit der Gründung des Büros 1989 gab es unterschiedliche Konstellationen der Partnerschaft. Eine Art Generationenwechsel hat nicht erst vor Kurzem stattgefunden, sondern kontinuierlich. Der Gründungsort Bern hängt als grosser Schwarzplan an der Bürowand, rot hineingesprenkelt sind die knapp 40 Projekte von GWJ in dieser Stadt. Zögerndes Schweigen nach der Frage, ob man sich als Berner Büro versteht. Ja, der Grossteil der Werke stehe tatsächlich hier und man sei dieser Stadt verbunden. «Viele von uns sind nicht aus Bern, doch wir identifizieren uns mit dieser Stadt und ihren Menschen.» Als lokales Architekturbüro verstehe man sich allerdings nicht.

2. Transformation

Ein Wettbewerbsgewinn für ein Bankgebäude an der Worblentalstrasse in Ittigen nahe Bern brachte 1991 den ersten Auftrag. Die Bank zog nie ein, stattdessen übernahmen Bundesbehörden die Räume. Heute, 30 Jahre nach Baubeginn, dürfen GWJ ihren Erstling ein weiteres Mal umbauen. 2024 gewann das Büro den Wettbewerb für die Transformation in ein Wohnhaus. Flexible Strukturen und einfache Konstruktion, Systemtrennung und Low-tech sind die Zutaten, die dem Haus immer wieder neue Leben ermöglichen – das hatten anfangs der Neunzigerjahre noch nicht viele Architekturbüros auf dem Schirm. Einfache, anpassbare Systeme ermöglichen es den Nutzenden, sich das Gebäude anzueignen, und geben auch Bedürfnissen Raum, die während des Baus noch gar nicht bekannt sind. All das führt auch zu einer gewissen Neutralität im Ausdruck. Benedikt Loderer schrieb zum ersten Wettbewerb: «Wo alle schreien, ist der Schweiger hörbar.»

Das aktuelle Umbauprojekt ist da mehr im Trend und verschweigt nicht seinen State of the Art: leichte Bauteile, Kreislauf, Re-use, das volle Programm. GWJ waren früh dran, die Zeit hat aufgeholt, GWJ machen weiter. Obwohl aufgestockt, mit neuer Fassade und Balkonen versehen, soll der Charakter des Ursprungsbaus noch durchscheinen, denn, so die Architekten, es sei zu einem Teil der Umgebung geworden. Das Haus als System ist wichtig, das Haus als Teil des grossen Ganzen noch wichtiger. Schönheit auch, sagen GWJ, denn Gebäude, die man schätzt, pflegt man.

3. Stadt

Städtebau ist nicht nur als Denkfigur zu Beginn eines jeden Projektes präsent, sondern auch als eigene Disziplin im Portfolio. Parallel zum ersten Auftrag in Ittigen nahm das frisch gegründete Büro an einem weltweit offenen städtebaulichen Ideenwettbewerb

GRASPING GWJ IN 7 TERMS

Axel Simon

1. Bern

An unremarkable office building on Nordring in Bern, perhaps a hundred years old. The GWJ architecture practice firm has occupied one of the floors for 25 years, ever since the publishing firm that used to be based there closed its printshop. When you step out of the lift, you find yourself right in the office. The open, almost empty space is framed by the glass of the meeting rooms. Models and material samples, books and magazines are stored on low shelves. Beyond the stairwell, visitors are surprised by a huge mushroom-shaped column, a vestige of the former printshop. Employees' workstations cluster around it, with project teams sitting together in groups. Focused hustle and bustle and striking diversity: many young people and different nationalities. "Well done, Selina!" congratulates the office's website on completing her apprenticeship and reports on the summer party featuring a pizza workshop.

GWJ is young, even though the practice is older than many of its employees. Their average age is 34. "We're not getting any older," say the four partners, who are supported in leadership by two associates. Since its foundation in 1989, the partnership structure has shifted several times. Instead of a kind of generational change, the transformation has been gradual. On the office wall hangs a large site plan of Bern, the city where the firm was founded, with GWJ's nearly 40 projects completed in the city marked in red. When asked whether they consider themselves a Bernese practice, there is a moment of hesitant silence. Yes, most of their work is indeed located here, and they feel connected to the city. "Many of us are not originally from Bern, but we identify with the city and its people." However, they do not regard themselves as a local architectural practice.

2. Transformation

The practice's first commission came in 1991 with a competition win for the construction of a bank building on Worblentalstrasse in Ittigen, near Bern. The bank never moved in; instead, federal authorities took over the space. Now, 30 years after construction began, GWJ has the opportunity to convert its first project again. In 2024, the practice won the competition to transform it into a residential building. Flexible structures and simple construction, system separation, and low-tech solutions are the ingredients that have allowed the building to take on new life, an approach that few architectural firms were considering in the early 1990s. Simple and adaptable systems enable users to make the building their own and also accommodate needs that were unknown at the time of construction. This approach also gives the building a certain neutrality in its architectural expression. Regarding the first competition, Benedikt Loderer wrote: "Where everyone shouts, the silent voice is heard."

The current renovation project is more in line with current trends, embracing its state-of-the-art approach: lightweight components, circularity, reuse, the full package. GWJ were ahead of their time; now time has caught up and GWJ keep going. Although the building is being raised and fitted with a new façade and balconies,the architects aim to preserve the character of the original structure, which has, in part, become a part of its surroundings. The building as a system is important, but as part of the larger whole, it is even more so. Beauty matters too, say GWJ, because buildings that are valued are also cared for.

mit 835 teilnehmenden Büros aus 44 Ländern teil. Für das Parlaments- und Regierungsviertel am Spreebogen in Berlin schlugen GWJ vor, die Regierungsgebäude in die weitergestrickte Blockrandstruktur einzubetten. Sie übersetzten die demokratische Staatsform in Städtebau und landeten damit auf dem 3. Rang – und in der öffentlichen Debatte.

GWJ machen Städtebau in einem umfassenden Sinn. Städtebau nicht verstanden als das Setzen von Baukörpern, sondern als ein Interesse an den Gegebenheiten des spezifischen Ortes – und an dem, was aus dem Bauen resultiert: dem Zusammenleben. Städtebau sei «Gestaltung eines guten Neben- und Miteinanders für alle». Im Zentrum stehen dabei die Übergänge und Schwellenräume – jenes Dazwischen, in dem Gemeinschaft, Alltag und Leben entstehen. Und wo zugleich Rückzug und Privatheit möglich bleiben sollten.

4. Milieu

Die Übersichtspläne in diesem Buch sind Luftbilder, keine Schwarzpläne. Pläne sind abstrakt, sie zeigen eine reduzierte, bereinigte Version eines Ortes. Bilder, Fotos zeigen mehr. «Unser Interesse misst sich an der Gesamtheit und Wirkung der gebauten, nicht der gedachten Architektur», schreiben GWJ in einer Notiz. Einfacher könnte man sagen: Sie sind keine Hardcore-Architekten, die um die Perfektion eines Details kämpfen, um ihre Vorstellung möglichst reine Wirklichkeit werden zu lassen. Es geht ihnen primär um den gestalteten Lebensraum, nicht um das gestaltete Objekt, das man Gebäude nennt. Es geht ihnen um die Stimmung des von ihnen veränderten Ortes.

Ein Begriff, der in unseren Gesprächen aber immer wieder fällt, ist «Milieu». Er bezeichnet das soziale Umfeld von Menschen, Tieren oder Pflanzen, hat heute aber einen altbackenen, ja anrüchigen Beigeschmack («Rotlichtmilieu»). Weil wir verlernt haben, auf das zu schauen, was da ist? GWJ versuchen dies. Sie suchen den offenen Austausch, zum Beispiel beim Bell-Areal in Kriens, wo sie nach einer Evaluation der Bedürfnisse die alte Produktionshalle und den neuen Quartiersplatz so vorbereiten, dass diese von den Bewohnerinnen und Bewohnern weitergestaltet werden können. Vieles soll möglich bleiben, gerade mit Blick auf die Schwellen- und Zwischenräume. Auch bei der integrativen Entwicklung eines 750 Meter langen Stadtraums in Wankdorf. Dort kooperieren sie mit vielen unterschiedlichen Planenden, was anstrengend sei, aber auch enorm bereichernd. «Pragmatischer Optimismus» ist auch so ein Begriff, der mir im Gedächtnis bleibt.

5. Marinade

Oder «marinieren». Das ist ein Vorgehen, das Martin Beutler von der Kulinarik in die Sozialraumplanung transferierte. Er ist ein Freund des Büros und arbeitet immer wieder mit ihm zusammen, auch in Wankdorf oder Kriens. Mariniert wird ein Projekt mit Gedanken, Eindrücken, Perspektiven, Kontexten. All dies verbindet sich miteinander und reift, um so den Möglichkeitsraum zu erkunden und zu erweitern. Ein schönes Bild für ein Projekt, das nicht einen einzelnen Koch kennt, sondern viele unterschiedliche. GWJ arbeiten oft und gern mit Partnern aller Disziplinen zusammen, und auch mit anderen Architekturbüros – nicht nur bei den oben genannten städtebaulichen Projekten, sondern zum Beispiel auch beim grossen Neubau des Inselspitals in Bern. Dort bestand das Team aus drei verschiedenen Büros. Zusammenarbeit bedeutet: auf Augenhöhe. Die Kooperation über fachliche Grenzen hinweg geschieht mit Blick aufs Ergebnis. Jede Disziplin soll dabei bewusst ins Gehege der anderen kommen, um mit frischem Blick den Entwurf zu bereichern.

Auch bei der preisgekrönten Siedlung Huebergass. Der vordere Teil des Grundstücks blieb unbebaut und wurde zum öffentlichen Park. Die Häuserzeilen richten ihre Eingänge und Balkone zu einer gemeinsamen Gasse mit Laden und Café; so entsteht

3. City

Urban planning does not only exist as a conceptual framework at the beginning of every project, but also as its own discipline within the firm's portfolio. Concurrently with its first commission in Ittigen, the newly established office entered a globally open urban design competition, with 835 participating firms from 44 different countries. For the parliamentary and government district at the Spreebogen in Berlin, GWJ proposed embedding the government buildings into the extended block-edge structure. They translated the democratic form of government into urban design, earning 3rd Place and a place in the public debate.

GWJ approaches urban planning in a comprehensive sense. Urban development is understood not as the placement of buildings it is about engaging with the unique conditions of each specific location – and in what emerges from building: coexistence. Urban plannig is, "the shaping of good coexistence and interaction for everyone". The focus lies on transitions and threshold spaces – the interstices where community, everyday routine and life itself take shape, while still allowing for retreat and privacy.

4. Milieu

The overview plans in this book are aerial photographs, not black-and-white plans. Plans are abstract; they present a reduced, simplified version of a location. Images and photographs reveal more. "Our interest is measured by the totality and impact of what is built, not of what is merely conceived," GWJ write in a note. Put more simply: they are not hardcore architects fighting for perfection in every detail in order to realize their ideas in the purest possible form. They are primarily concerned with the designed living space, not the designed object that we call a building. What matters to them is the atmosphere of the place they transform.

One term that comes up repeatedly in our conversations is "milieu". It refers to the social environment of people, animals or plants, but today has an old-fashioned, even slightly dubious connotation ("red-light milieu"). Is it perhaps because we have forgotten how to look at what is already there? GWJ try to do exactly that. They seek open exchange, for example at the Bell site in Kriens, where, after evaluating needs, they are preparing the old production hall and the new neighbourhood square in a way that can be further shaped by the residents themselves. Much is meant to remain possible, especially with regard to threshold and in-between spaces. The same also applies to the integrative development of a 750-metre-long urban space in Wankdorf, where they cooperate with many different planners, which is demanding but also enormously enriching. "Pragmatic optimism" is another expression that sticks with me.

5. Marinade

Or "to marinate". This is a method that Martin Beutler transferred from the culinary world to social spatial planning. A friend of the practice, he collaborates with it regularly, including in Wankdorf and Kriens. A project is marinated with ideas, impressions, perspectives and contexts. All of these elements blend and mature, allowing the scope of potential to be explored and expanded. It is a beautiful image for a project that does not have a single chef, but many different ones. GWJ often and gladly works with partners from all disciplines, as well as with other architectural practices – not only in the urban planning projects mentioned above, but also, for example, in the major new construction of the Inselspital in Bern, where the team consisted of three different practices.

Dichte. Solche Entwürfe entwickeln sich aus Erzählungen heraus. Oder, wie in diesem Fall, aus der Vorstellung einer Geräuschkulisse, die die bauliche und soziale Dichte vorab evozierte. Und heute höre es sich genauso an, sagen GWJ: ein Brodeln von 300 Leuten auf engstem Raum.

6. Realität

Der Blick aufs «unsaubere» Milieu, das «Marinieren» der Projekte mit unterschiedlichen Einflüssen – man könnte das Realismus nennen. Kein malerischer Realismus wie bei den Zürcher Analogen, sondern eine Offenheit gegenüber den Einflüssen, zu denen das Vorhandene und die Aufgabenstellung gehören, aber auch Vorschriften, Normen und Standards. Offenheit gegenüber der Bauherrschaft, Offenheit gegenüber dem Resultat eines Prozesses mit vielen Beteiligten. Architektur machen, das erfordere eine paradoxe Mischung aus Genauigkeit und Unbestimmtheit. Die Unsicherheit, nicht zu wissen, was man bekommt, das müsse man aushalten können.

Zum Realismus gehört auch eine ökonomische Kompetenz. GWJ übernehmen oft Gesamtplanungsaufgaben und damit Verantwortung – selbst die 80 000 Quadratmeter des Inselspitalgebäudes entstanden ohne Totalunternehmer. Gute, professionelle Prozesse, Abliefern im Zeit- und Kostenrahmen, auch das gehöre zur Baukultur. «Gutes Wirtschaften». Ökonomie ist wichtig – auch eine Ökonomie der Mittel, der bestmögliche Einsatz der verfügbaren Ressourcen und das Auskommen mit dem Vorhandenen. In der Huebergasse zeigt das ein ganz simples Detail: Abflussrinnen im Boden der Gasse leiten das Oberflächenwasser zu den Bäumen; diese Rinnen sind nicht aufwändig gemauert, sondern einfach in den Asphalt gefräst.

7. Das erste Mal

GWJ sind nicht, wie viele andere Büros, spezialisiert. Sie machen vieles, Städtebau und Umbauten, bauen Wohngebäude und Spitäler, Bildungs- und Verwaltungsgebäude. Da ist sie wieder, die Offenheit, auch Neugierde auf neue Bauaufgaben und Gegenden – eben: Man sei ja kein «Berner Büro». «Am offenen Wettbewerb in Zermatt haben wir teilgenommen, weil wir mal eine Schule entwerfen wollten.» Sie haben gewonnen. Heute steht die Schule.

Das junge Traditionsbüro GWJ Architektur transformiert sich stetig. Es entdeckt immer wieder neue Arbeitsfelder. Es arbeitet leidenschaftlich mit anderen zusammen und schon lange an Themen, die heute aktueller sind, denn je: Kreislaufwirtschaft, Umgang mit Bestehendem, Ganzheitlichkeit. Themen, die in der Fachwelt lange – zu lange – keine waren und die noch immer zu langsam umgesetzt werden. Die Architekten freuen sich, dass diese Themen nun mehr und mehr im Fokus der Bauherrschaften stehen. Vor allem die jüngeren Mitarbeiterinnen und Mitarbeiter bringen viel Wissen darüber ein. Und das bereichert die Arbeit rund um die riesige Pilzstütze am Nordring in Bern.

Collaboration means working at eye level, while cooperation across professional boundaries is guided by the result. Each discipline is meant to consciously enter the territory of the others, enriching the design with a fresh perspective.

This was also the case with the award-winning Huebergasse housing development. The front area of the property was left undeveloped and converted into a public park. The rows of houses orientate their entrances and balconies toward a shared alley with a shop and café, creating a sense of density. Such designs grow out of narratives. Or, as in this case, from the idea of a soundscape that anticipated the structural and social density. Today, GWJ explains, it sounds exactly like that: the buzz of 300 people inhabiting a dense, shared space.

6. Reality

The attention to the "messy" milieu, the "marinating" of projects with diverse influences – one could call this realism. Not a picturesque realism like that of the "Zurich Analogues", but an openness to all the factors at play: the existing conditions, the task at hand, as well as regulations, codes and standards. Openness towards the client, openness towards the outcome of a process involving many participants. Architecture requires a paradoxical mixture of precision and indeterminacy. You need to be able to cope with the uncertainty of not knowing exactly what the result will be.

Realism also requires economic competence. GWJ often assume overall planning tasks and thus responsibility; even the 80,000 square metres of the Inselspital were built without a general contractor. Good professional processes and delivery within time and budget are also part of our building culture. "Good practice". Economy is important – including an economy of means, efficiently utilising resources and working with what is available. Huebergasse illustrates this principle through a simple detail: drainage channels in the floor of the alleyway guide surface water to the trees; they are achieved not with elaborate masonry, but by cutting gutters into the asphalt.

7. Our first time

Unlike many other practices, GWJ is not a specialist firm. It carries out a wide range of projects, including urban development and conversions, residential buildings, hospitals, and research, educational and administrative complexes. Here it is again, the openness, even curiosity, toward new building types and contexts, after all, they are not simply a "Bernese practice". "We entered the open competition in Zermatt because we wanted the chance to design a school," they recall. They won. Today, the school stands.

The young, yet established firm GWJ is constantly evolving. It is always discovering new fields of work. It collaborates passionately with others and has long been working on topics that are more relevant today than ever before: circular economy, dealing with existing structures and holistic design. These are topics that the professional world long ignored, too long, and that are still being implemented far too slowly. The architects are pleased that these issues are increasingly being addressed. The younger generation, in particular, brings substantial knowledge to the table, enriching the work around the massive mushroom-shaped column at Nordring in Bern.

ERSCHWINGLICH UND INKLUSIV HUEBERGASS UND STADTTEILPARK, BERN

Holligen geht neue Wege im genossenschaftlichen Wohnen. Anstelle eines Familiengartenareals sind über 100 preisgünstige, integrative Wohnungen und im Gegenzug ein Quartierpark entstanden. Wie werden die Menschen hier zusammenleben? Welche Instrumente und Räume fördern dieses Zusammenleben? Aus diesen Fragen erwuchs die Kernidee des Entwurfs: Eine Wohngasse im Anschluss an die Wohngebiete schafft Platz für einen grosszügigen, der Öffentlichkeit zugewandten Park.

Dank ihrer Innenorientierung ist die Gasse die pulsierende Mittelachse der Siedlung. Hier kreuzen sich die Wege, von hier aus sind Wohnungen, Gemeinschaftsräume und das Quartiercafé erschlossen. Verschiedene Öffentlichkeitsgrade erfordern das bewusste Kultivieren der Schnittstellen: Die Wohngebäude wenden sich mit ihren Balkonen und Aussentreppen zur Gasse hin und vom Park ab – und zollen so dem öffentlichen Raum Respekt. Der Austausch zwischen Genossenschaft, Nachbarschaft und Park konzentriert sich an ausgewählten Plätzen am Übergang der Räume.

Fundament dieser Gestaltung war eine kollaborative Arbeitsweise: Vor der Objektplanung stand die integrative Quartierplanung, vor dem gestalteten Raum der partizipative Prozess. Die planerische Wertschätzung der Gemeinschaft hat eine hohe Wertschätzung der Gemeinschaft für die Planung generiert. Was geschätzt wird, wird gepflegt – so wird Wertschätzung zum Nachhaltigkeitsfaktor.

AFFORDABLE AND INCLUSIVE HUEBERGASS AND DISTRICT PARK, BERN

Holligen is breaking new ground in co-operative living. Instead of a traditional family-orientated garden development, over 100 affordable, socially inclusive apartments, along with a community park, were built. How would people live together here? What instruments and spaces could support this community? These questions led to the key idea behind the design: a residential alleyway between housing blocks, which provided enough space for a large park open to the public.

The alleyway is the lively central axis of the development thanks to its inward orientation. This is where pathways meet, and from here apartments, common rooms and the neighbourhood café can be reached. The varying levels of accessibility necessitate deliberate consideration in the design of transition spaces. The residential buildings, with their balconies and outdoor staircases, are orientated towards the alley and away from the park, thereby acknowledging and respecting the public space. Interaction between the co-operative, the local neighbourhood and the park occurs within specific locations at the transition between the different spaces.

Collaboration formed the foundation of the design process: before the building planning was conceived, there was inclusive neighbourhood planning; before spatial design, there was a participative process. The engagement of the planning team with the community fostered a deep appreciation for the planning process and team within the community. What is genuinely valued tends to be preserved – thus community appreciation becomes a sustainability factor.

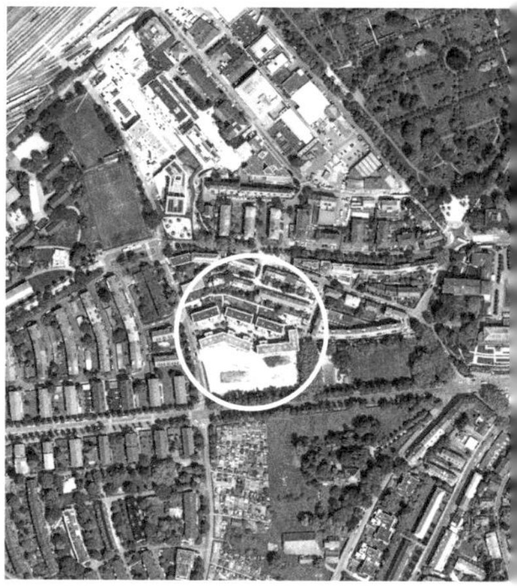

Investoren- und Projektwettbewerb: 2017, 1. Rang
Realisierung: 2019–2021
Bauherrschaft: Wohnbaugenossenschaft «Wir sind Stadtgarten», Bern
Kooperation:
GWJ Architektur AG, Bern
ORT AG, Zürich
Soziale Plastik, Bern

Investor and project competition: 2017, 1st Place
Construction: 2019–2021
Client: Wohnbaugenossenschaft "Wir sind Stadtgarten", Bern
Cooperation:
GWJ Architektur AG, Bern
ORT AG, Zurich
Soziale Plastik, Bern

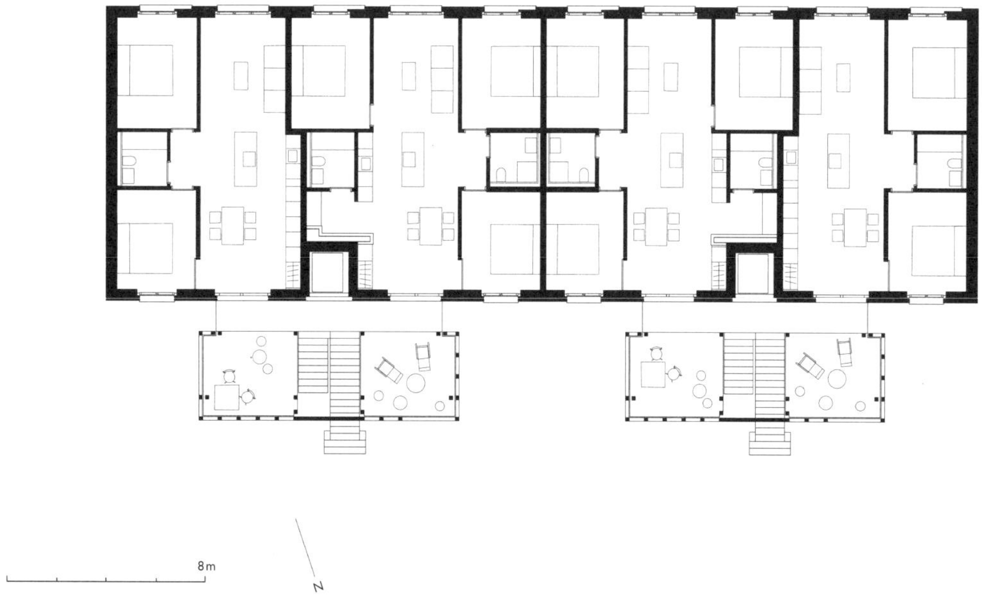

25 m

N
20 m

DAS POTENZIAL DER SUBSTANZ
AREAL GURTENBRAUEREI, WABERN

THE POTENTIAL OF THE BUILDING FABRIC
GURTEN BREWERY, WABERN

Die ehemalige Bierbrauerei Gurten hat am nördlichen Gurtenhang ein Stück gebaute Industriegeschichte hinterlassen. Historische Gebäude haben sich mit jüngeren industriellen Strukturen zu einer pittoresken Kulisse verbunden. Die strategisch und verkehrlich günstige Lage, die Nähe zur Stadt und zur Landschaft und der überwältigende Blick auf Bern boten beste Voraussetzungen für eine Revitalisierung und Umnutzung.

Der Prozess erforderte eine sorgfältige Balance zwischen Bewahren und Erneuern: Die zwei wichtigsten Erkenntnisse aus der Analyse wurden zur konzeptionellen Leitlinie: Die kleineren Gewerbebetriebe sind essenziell für die Ausstrahlung des Standorts; und der sehr unterschiedliche denkmalpflegerische Wert der Bausubstanz erfordert eine multiperspektivische Beurteilung.

Die interdisziplinäre Interessenabwägung führte zu einer Kaskade von Erhalt, Umnutzung und Neubau. Vergangenheit und Zukunft sind zusammengewachsen. Neuer Wohn- und Arbeitsraum belebt das Areal; Gewerbebetriebe finden dank einfachster Sanierungen erschwinglichen Raum in den Altbauten. Die Geschichte des Ortes lebt nicht nur in der Mischung aus zeitgenössischer und historischer Architektur, sondern auch in der Nutzung weiter.

The former Gurten brewery left behind a piece of industrial history on the northern Gurtenhang hillside. Historical buildings and recent industrial structures have come together creating a picturesque scenery. With its attractive, strategic and easily accessible location, near both the city and the countryside, along with a magnificent view of Bern, it offered ideal preconditions for its revitalisation and conversion.

The process required a careful balance between preservation and renovation. The two most important findings from the analysis became the design concept guidelines: the smaller businesses were essential for the attractiveness of the location, while the widely varying preservation status of the building fabric required a multi-perspective assessment.

The interdisciplinary weighing up of interests led to a cascade of preservation, adaptive reuse and new construction. The past and future have grown together. New housing and working spaces have revitalised the area; small businesses have found affordable space in the old buildings thanks to simple renovations. The history of the site lives on not only in the mixture of contemporary and historical structures, but also in its mixed-use architecture.

Arealentwicklung: 2004
Testplanung: 2005–2007
Studienauftrag: 2008
Bauherrschaft: PSP Swiss Property

Area development: 2004
Test planning: 2005–2007
Contracted study: 2008
Client: PSP Swiss Property

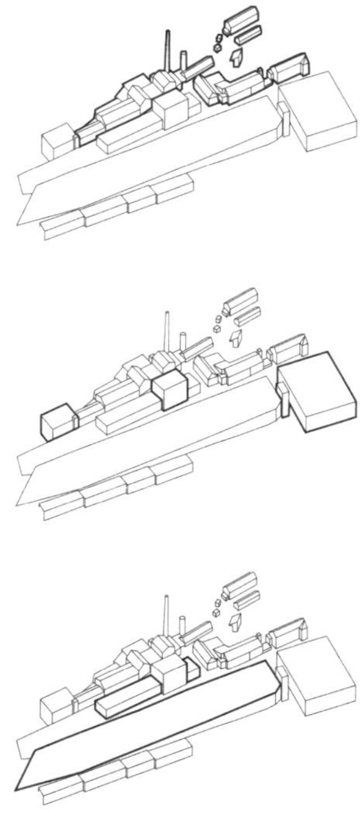

Instand stellen / sanieren / neu bauen
Preservation / Conversion / New construction

VERDICHTEN UND BEWAHREN
WOHNEN IM PARK, ITTIGEN

DENSIFICATION AND PRESERVATION
HOUSING IN A PARK, ITTIGEN

Die weitläufige Wohnsiedlung aus den 1980er Jahren wird von der Anwohnerschaft geliebt. Ihr Konzept offener Freiraumringe zwischen konzentrisch platzierten Gebäuden ist auch das Leitmotiv für die Erweiterung und Sanierung.

Die Transformation ist behutsam, doch wirkungsvoll: Der bestehende Wohnraum – und seine Mieterschaft – können bleiben. Einzelne Neubauten an den Kreuzungspunkten der Wege unterstreichen das konzentrische Bebauungsprinzip und akzentuieren wichtige Orientierungspunkte. Die Bestandsgebäude werden um zwei bis drei Geschosse aufgestockt, die darunter liegenden Wohnungen saniert und energetisch optimiert. Zusätzlich zum bestehenden entsteht so neuer, zeitgemässer Wohnraum.

Unterschiedliche Gebäudehöhen und vertikale Schichtungen schaffen eine differenzierte Massstäblichkeit. Die ressourcenschonende Kombination von Bestand und Neubau erweitert das Wohnungsangebot, die flexiblen Grundstrukturen der neuen Wohnungen steigern die Vielfalt hinsichtlich Schnitt, Grösse, Standard und Preis. Im Freiraum bleiben der Gartenstadtcharakter und ein Grossteil der alten Bäume erhalten, eine feinere Differenzierung der bislang homogenen Gestaltung macht diese besser nutzbar und stärkt die Siedlung als Sozialraum.

Alteingesessene und neue Bewohnerinnen und Bewohner, verschiedene Wohnformen und Mietpreise fügen sich zu einer neuen, robusten Vielfalt.

The extensive housing estate from the 1980s is loved by local residents. Its concept of circular open spaces between concentrically positioned buildings was also the theme for the extension and refurbishment project.

The transformation is subtle, yet effective: the existing housing blocks – and their residents – can remain there. Single new buildings at the intersections of the footpaths will reinforce the concentric development principle and mark important points of orientation. Two to three storeys will be added to the existing buildings, while the apartments below will be renovated and optimised in terms of energy efficiency. The result will be new, contemporary, additional housing.

Different building heights and vertical layering aim to achieve a differentiated scale. The resource-saving combination of existing and new buildings will expand the housing offer, while the flexible basic structures of the new apartments will increase diversity in terms of layout, size, standard and price. In outdoor spaces, the urban garden character and most of the old trees will be preserved, while the previously homogeneous design's subtle differentiations throughout make it more usable and strengthen the estate as a social space.

Long-established and new residents, various forms of housing and rental prices combine to create a new, robust diversity.

Studienauftrag auf Einladung
für Generalplanerteams: 2021, 1. Preis
Bauherrschaft: Allianz Suisse AG
Kooperation:
GWJ Architektur AG, Bern
Chaves Biedermann GmbH, Basel

Invitation contracted study for general planning teams: 2021, 1st Prize
Client: Allianz Suisse AG
Cooperation:
GWJ Architektur AG, Bern
Chaves Biedermann GmbH, Basel

N
40 m

IDENTITÄT STATT ABRISS
UNTERMATTWEG 8, BERN

IDENTITY INSTEAD OF DEMOLITION
UNTERMATTWEG 8, BERN

Der Hauptsitz der Galenica, ein Stahlbau aus den 1960er Jahren, wird saniert und teilweise umgenutzt. Seine Weiterentwicklung ist Teil eines umfassenden Nachhaltigkeitskonzepts. Das schlägt sich nicht nur im wertschätzenden Umgang mit dem Bestand nieder, sondern auch in der vorausschauenden Berücksichtigung der Quartierentwicklung rundum.

Die grundlegende Gebäudestruktur aus Sockel und Längsbau bleibt erhalten. Im Sockel, der ehemaligen Produktionshalle, wird künftig gewohnt. Der Turm, das bisherige Bürogebäude, bleibt Firmenhauptsitz. Die nötige und verträgliche Eingriffstiefe wird dort definiert, wo die grössten Veränderungen stattfinden: im Sockelbau. Hier sind für die Wohnnutzung ein neuer Innenhof und partielle Aufstockungen nötig.

Die Gestaltung und Materialisierung der neuen Elemente orientiert sich an der industriellen Geschichte des Gebäudes und spurt bereits den zu erwartenden Wandel im Quartier vor – unter anderem mit einer öffentlichen Durchwegung auf Bodenebene. Wie Bauteile und -materialien im konkreten Fall wiederverwendet oder recycelt werden können, wird im Moment erprobt. Einfache, robuste Konstruktionen, vereinheitlichte Systeme und konsequente Systemtrennung halten Möglichkeiten für weitere Nutzungsänderungen offen.

The headquarters of Galenica, a steel structure building dating back to the 1960s, is being renovated and partially repurposed. Its ongoing development is part of a comprehensive sustainability concept. This is reflected not only in the careful handling of the existing building, but also in the forward-looking approach to neighbourhood development.

The main building structure, formed by a base and a longitudinal building, will be preserved. The base, the former manufacturing hall, will be used for residential purposes. The tower, the previous office building, will remain as the company headquarters. The required and sustainable depth of intervention is defined with regard to where the greatest changes will take place: in the base building. Here, a new inner courtyard and partial extensions are required for the residential use.

The design and materialisation of the new components are based on the industrial history of the building and already anticipate the transformation to be expected in the neighbourhood – including a public walkway at ground level. How components and materials can be reused or recycled in specific cases is currently being researched. Simple, robust constructions, standardised systems and a consistent system separation provide opportunities for further use changes.

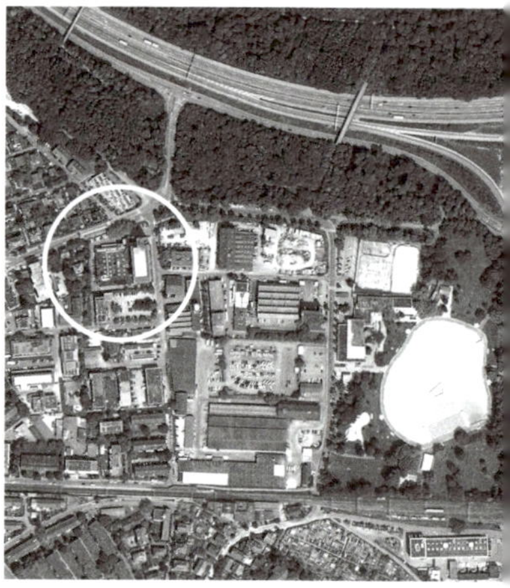

Entwurf: 2022
Realisierung: 2024–2030
Bauherrschaft: UBS Fund Management (Switzerland) AG
Kooperation:
GWJ Architektur AG, Bern
ORT AG, Zürich

Design: 2022
Construction: 2024–2030
Client: UBS Fund Management (Switzerland) AG
Cooperation:
GWJ Architektur AG, Bern
ORT AG, Zurich

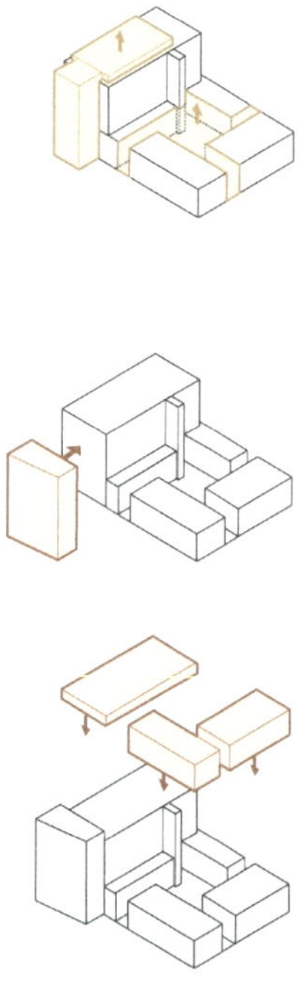

Rückbau / Anbau / Aufstockung
Demolition / Extension / Heightening

1. Dach mit Kombination aus Photovoltaikanlage und intensiver Begrünung zur optimalen Sonnenernte und als Lebensgrundlage verschiedener Pflanzen und Kleintiere.
Roof with a combination of a photovoltaic system and intensive greenery for ideal sun yields and as a habitat for various plants and small animals.

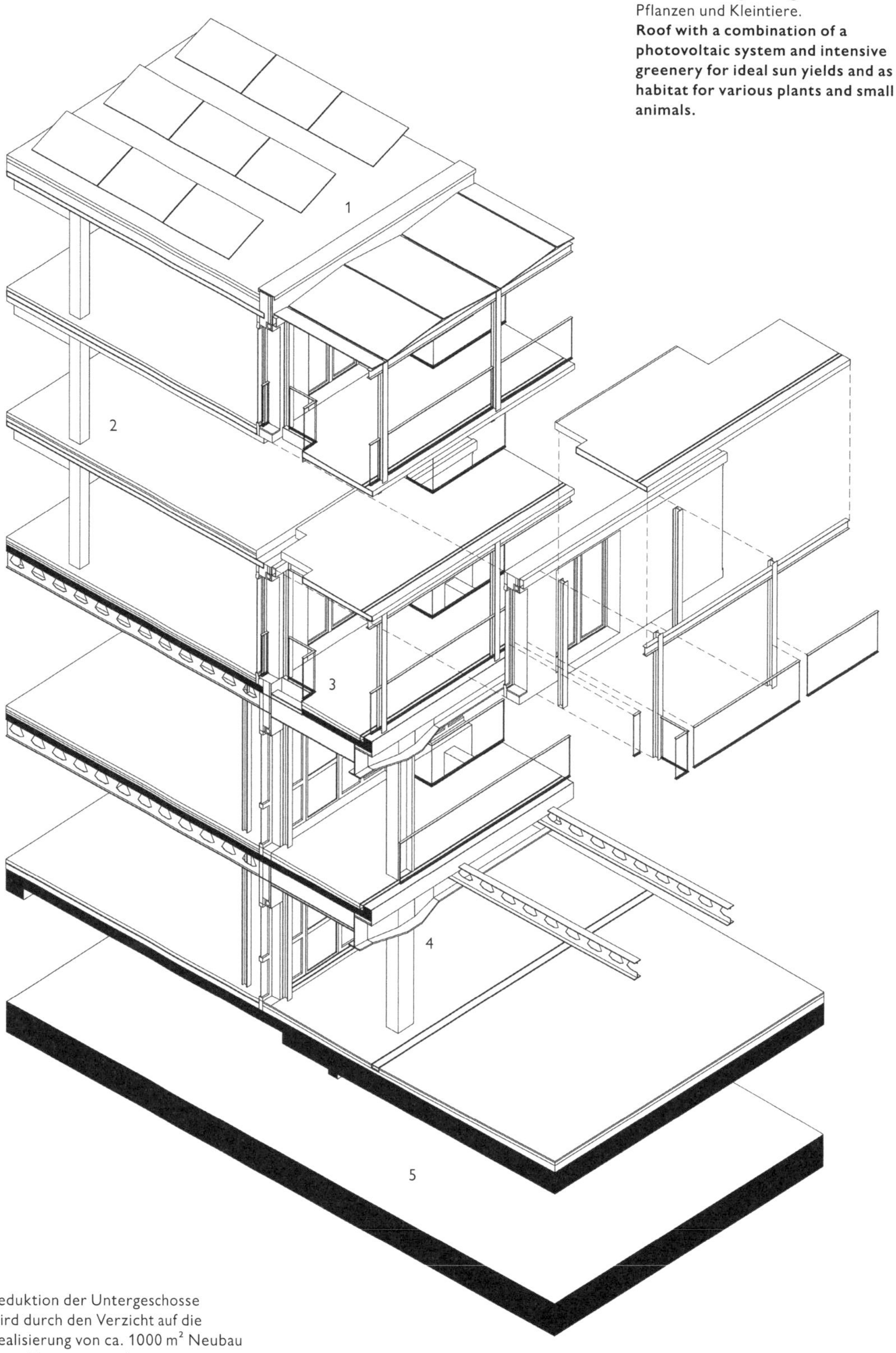

2. Aufstockungen in Holz- und Trockenbauweise führen zu effizienter, ressourcenschonender Lastabtragung und systemgetrennten Lösungen.
Heightening in wood and dry construction methods leads to efficient, resource-saving load transfers and solutions with separate systems.

3. Laubengang mit Stahlprofilen und vorfabrizierten Betonelementen. Additives Befestigungsprinzip.
Walkway with steel profiles and prefabricated concrete elements. Additive bracing principle.

4. Maximaler Erhalt der bestehenden Stahlstruktur und des Rohbaus führt zur Einsparung von Ressourcen und Bewahrung von Identität.
Maximum preservation of the existing steel structure and the shell structure saves resources and preserves the development's identity.

5. Reduktion der Untergeschosse wird durch den Verzicht auf die Realisierung von ca. 1000 m^2 Neubau unter Terrain erreicht.
Reducing the basement floor is achieved by deciding against constructing approx. 1,000 m^2 of new underground building space.

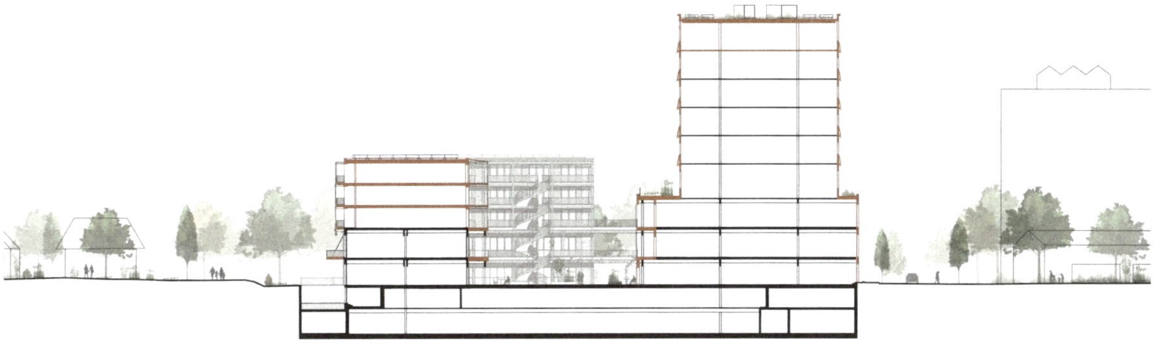

25 m

■ Bestand
Existing structure

■ Neubau
New development

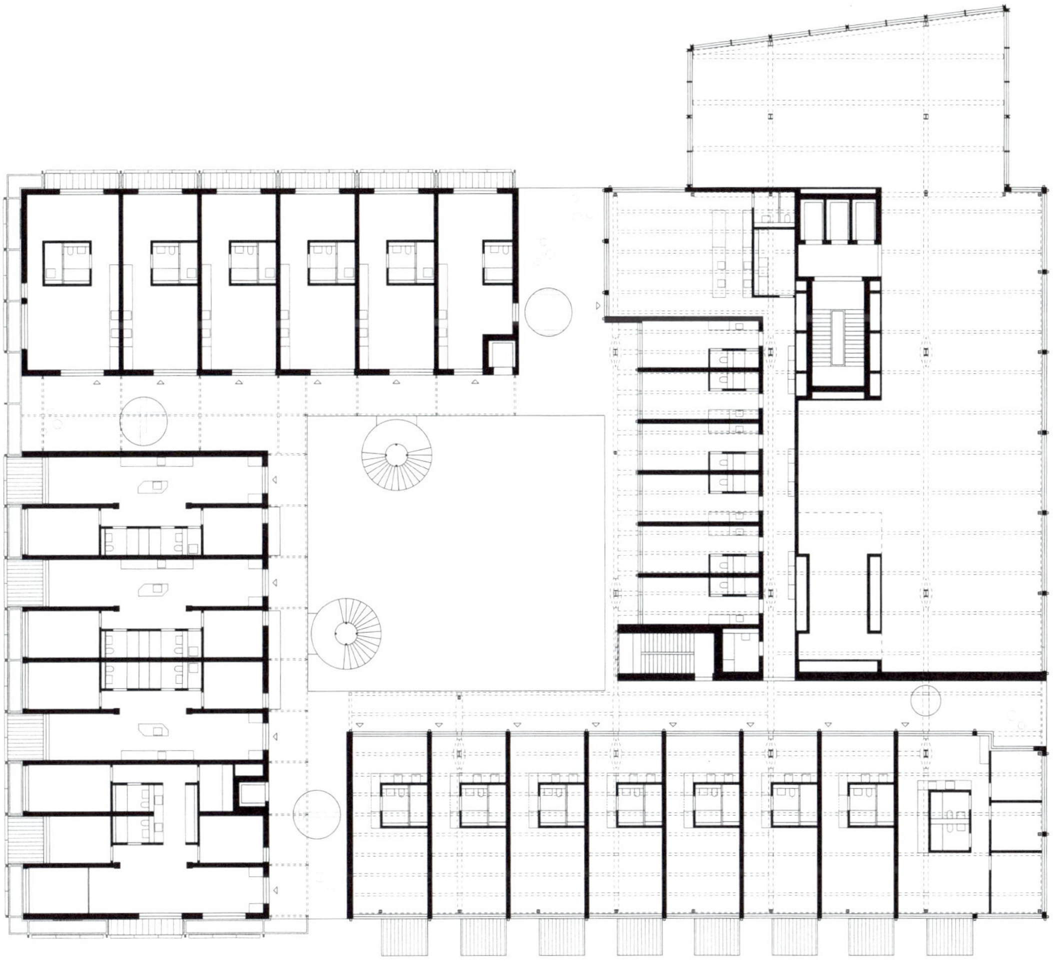

15 m

N

FLEXIBILITÄT AUF DEM PRÜFSTAND
WORBLENTALSTRASSE 68, ITTIGEN

FLEXIBILITY TESTED
WORBLENTALSTRASSE 68, ITTIGEN

Taugt ein Verwaltungsgebäude auch als Wohnbau? Schon 1998 hat GWJ sich beim Bau des Bürohauses maximale Wandlungsfähigkeit auf die Fahne geschrieben. So ist dank additivem Konstruktionsprinzip und konsequenter Systemtrennung nun eine umfassende Transformation des Lowtech-Gebäudes möglich: Aus 500 nicht mehr benötigten Arbeitsplätzen wird Wohnraum für 300 Personen.

Die Aufstockung und Erweiterung des Baukörpers in Richtung Freiraum integriert das Gebäude noch besser in die Nachbarschaft. Seine parkartige Umgebung bildet die Adresse und verbindet den Bau mit seinem Umfeld. Nach innen wird der bestehende Hof zum zentralen Treffpunkt für die Bewohnerinnen und Bewohner. Spielflächen unter der überdachten Erdgeschosszone und zusätzliche Höfe auf verschiedenen Ebenen fördern die Begegnung und das Zusammenleben der neuen Bewohnerschaft.

Der Umbau setzt – angesichts der frühen Umnutzung auch aus ökonomischer Notwendigkeit – auf eine umfassende Nachhaltigkeit: Aus dem Bestand heraus entstehen 25 Prozent mehr Nutzfläche, viele sekundäre Bauteile können weiterverwendet oder adaptiert werden. Das ist nicht nur ökologisch, sondern auch ökonomisch sinnvoll und ermöglicht zudem hochwertigen Raum für ein gutes Zusammenleben. Das bekannte Gebäude erhält eine neue, vielversprechende Zukunft.

Is an office building also suitable as housing? Back in 1998, GWJ set itself the goal of maximising adaptability when constructing the office building. Thanks to the modular design concept and consistent system separation, a complex transformation of the low-tech building is now possible: 500 workstations that are no longer needed are turned into living accommodation for 300 people.

The addition of storeys and building extension towards the open space helps to integrate the building even better into the neighbourhood. Its park-like surroundings form the building's address and connect it to its environment. On the inside, the existing courtyard becomes the central meeting point for residents. Play(ground) areas under the covered ground floor zone and additional courtyards on various levels foster encounters and socialising among the new residents.

In view of the building's early conversion and the resulting economic necessities, the transformation also focuses on comprehensive sustainability: 25% more usable space is created from the existing structures, while many secondary building elements could be reused or adapted. This is not only ecologically, but also economically viable and provides a high-quality space for community living. The well-known building is being given a new, promising future.

Studienauftrag: 2023, 1. Preis
Bauherrschaft: Pensionskasse des Bundes PUBLICA
Kooperation:
GWJ Architektur AG, Bern
Chaves Biedermann GmbH, Basel

Contracted study: 2023, 1st Prize
Client: Pensionskasse des Bundes PUBLICA
Cooperation:
GWJ Architektur AG, Bern
Chaves Biedermann GmbH, Basel

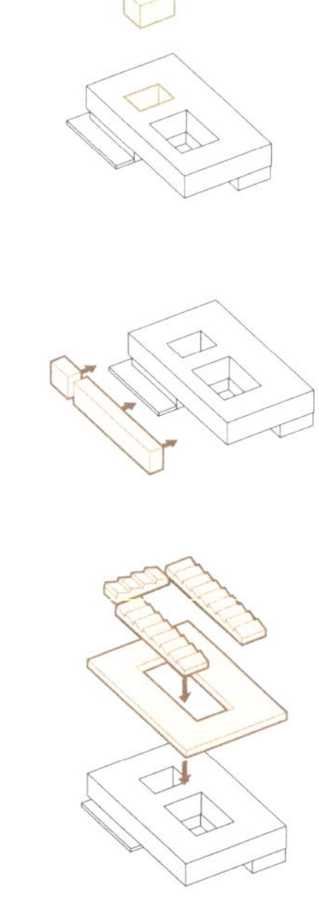

Rückbau / Anbau / Aufstockung
Demolition / Extension / Heightening

Talgutzentrum
tBiodiversität
Dachgarten
Nachhaltig wohnen
PV, Re-Use, Regenwasser
Townhouses
Das Dorf auf dem Dach
Liegewiese
Dachoase
Sonne tanken
im Winter
Hofoase
Spendet Schatten
im Sommer
Wohnhof
Ateliers
Ateliers
Gartenhaus
Eingangshalle
Click and collect
Packet-Anlage
Spielplatz
Für die Kleinen
Velotreff
Verweilen und beobachten
Plattform
Spielplatz
Biotop
Park
Spielwiese
Für Spiel und Sport
Bahnstrasse

25 m

■ Bestand
Existing structure

■ Neubau
New development

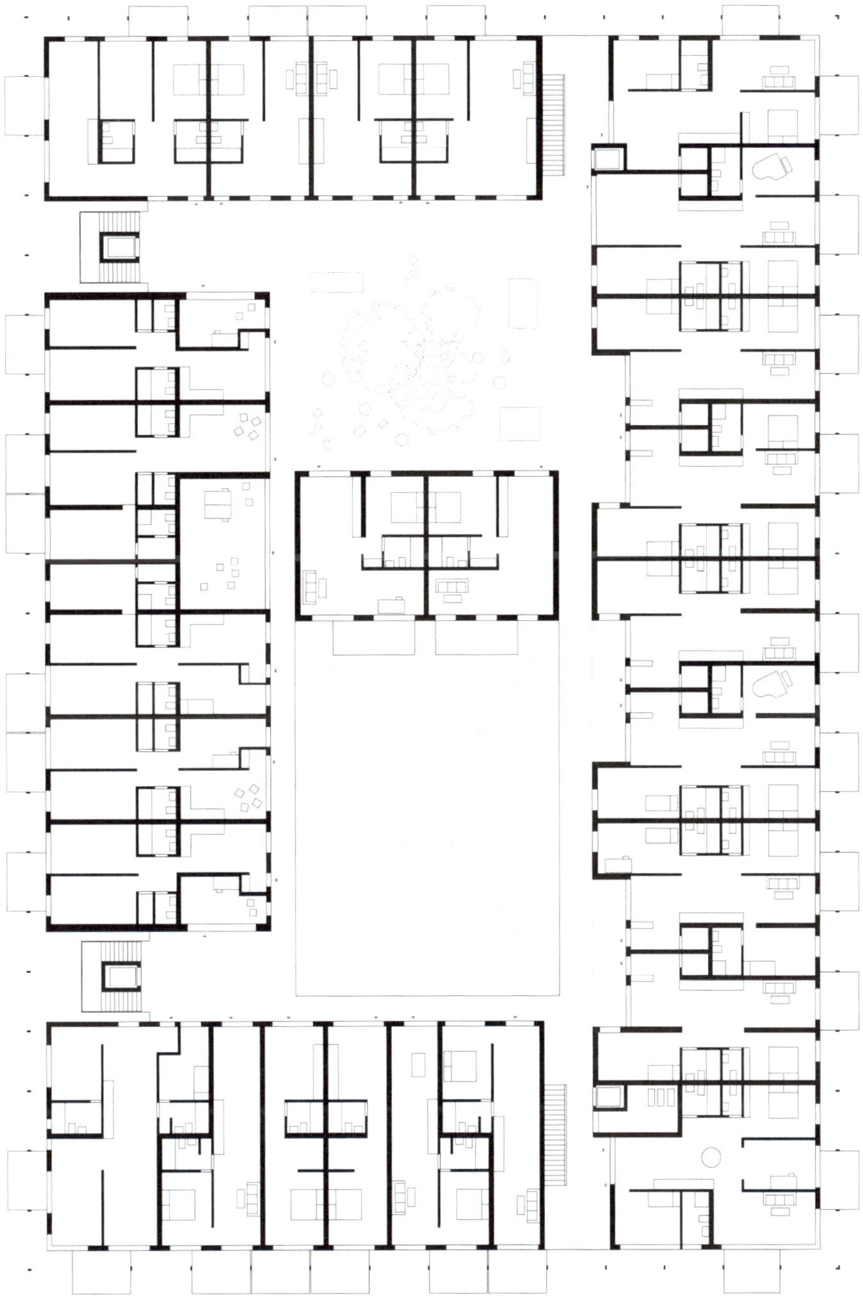

N

15 m

MODERNISIERUNG EINER IKONE
TAUBENHALDE 16, BERN

MODERNISING AN ICON
TAUBENHALDE 16, BERN

Das Areal der Schweizerischen Bundesverwaltung am Rande des UNESCO-Welterbe-Perimeters steht vor einer anspruchsvollen Sanierung. Es gilt, die raue Architektursprache aus den 1970er Jahren mit den aktuellen Nachhaltigkeitszielen des Bundes in Einklang zu bringen.

Das klare Gebäuderaster setzt den Rahmen für die neue Raumorganisation. Zeitgemässe Arbeitsräume, die den hohen Anforderungen an Sicherheit, Daten- und Persönlichkeitsschutz gerecht werden, fügen sich dank intensiver Variantenabwägung optimal darin ein. Zentraler Bestandteil der Sanierung ist zudem ein umfassendes Klimamassnahmenpaket. Auch in der Freiraumgestaltung sind ökologische und siedlungsklimatische Anforderungen im Geist des Originalkonzepts mit den Nutzungs- und Sicherheitsbedürfnissen zu verknüpfen. Die Wiederverwertung von Materialien und Bauteilen dient nicht nur der Nachhaltigkeit, sondern auch der Wahrung der schlichten, repräsentativen Ästhetik der baulichen Ikone.

Die Schärfung der Qualitäten des Bestands, seine bauliche Sanierung und die Optimierung der Arbeitsbedingungen in einem Konzept zu vereinen, war angesichts laufender Veränderungen am Anforderungskatalog ein intensiver Aushandlungs- und Optimierungsprozess mit allen Fachbereichen und Betroffenen. Dieser Prozess ist wesentlicher Teil der Lösung.

The area around the Swiss Federal Administration, on the edge of the UNESCO World Heritage perimeter, requires demanding renovation measures. The aim is to harmonise the coarse architectural language of the 1970s with contemporary aims of sustainability in Switzerland.

The clear building grid forms the framework of the new spatial organisation. Contemporary workrooms that fulfil the high demands with respect to security, data protection and privacy are ideally integrated through the intensive consideration of different variations. A key element of the renovation is also a comprehensive package of climate-related measures. The design of the open spaces combine ecological and urban climate requirements with use and safety demands following the original concept. The reuse of materials and building elements not only supports sustainability, but also preserves the simple, refined aesthetics of the iconic building.

Due to ongoing changes in the requirements catalogue, an intensive negotiation and optimisation process with all departments and participants was required to combine the enhancing of the qualities of the existing building, renovating its fabric and optimising working conditions in a single, combined concept. This process played a key role in the solution.

Planerwahlverfahren: 2020, 1. Rang
Realisierung: 2026–2029
Bauherrschaft: Bundesamt für Bauten und Logistik (BBL)
Kooperation:
GWJ Architektur AG, Bern
CO. Architekten AG, Bern

Planning selection process: 2020, 1st Place
Construction: 2026–2029
Client: Bundesamt für Bauten und Logistik (BBL)
Cooperation:
GWJ Architektur AG, Bern
CO. Architekten AG, Bern

1. Dach mit Kombination aus Photovoltaikanlage und intensiver Begrünung zur optimalen Sonnenernte und als Lebensgrundlage verschiedener Pflanzen und Kleintiere.
Roof with a combination of a photovoltaic system and intensive greenery for ideal sun yields and as a habitat for various plants and small animals.

2. Innenwände können in jedem Raster an die Fassade anschliessen für die maximale Flexibilität in der Grundrisskonzeption.
The interior wall can be connected to the façade in any grid to ensure maximum flexibility for the floor-plan concept.

3. Horizontale Photovoltaikanlage an den ertragreichen Fassaden führt zu maximalem Sonnenertrag und schützt gleichzeitig vor Überhitzung und Schlagregen.
The horizontal photovoltaic system on the high-yield façades leads to maximum sun yields and also provides protection from overheating and driving rain.

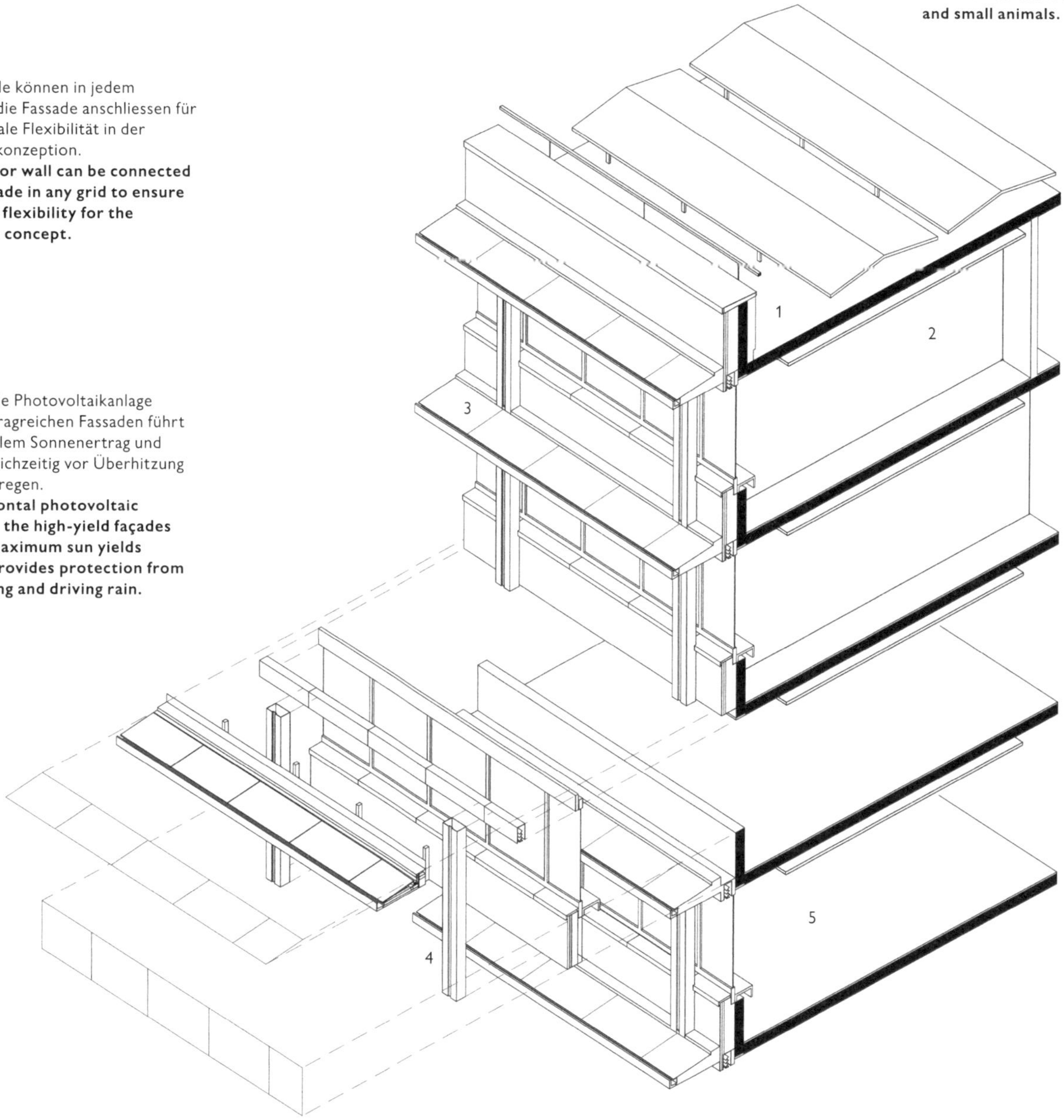

4. Vertikale Lisenen dienen der Erschliessung der Photovoltaikanlage und der Entwässerung und gliedern die grossen Fassadenflächen.
Vertical pilaster strips are used to connect the photovoltaic system and for drainage, while also structuring the large areas of the façade.

5. Maximaler Erhalt der bestehenden Betonstruktur führt zur Einsparung von Ressourcen.
Preserving as much of the existing concrete structure as possible saves resources.

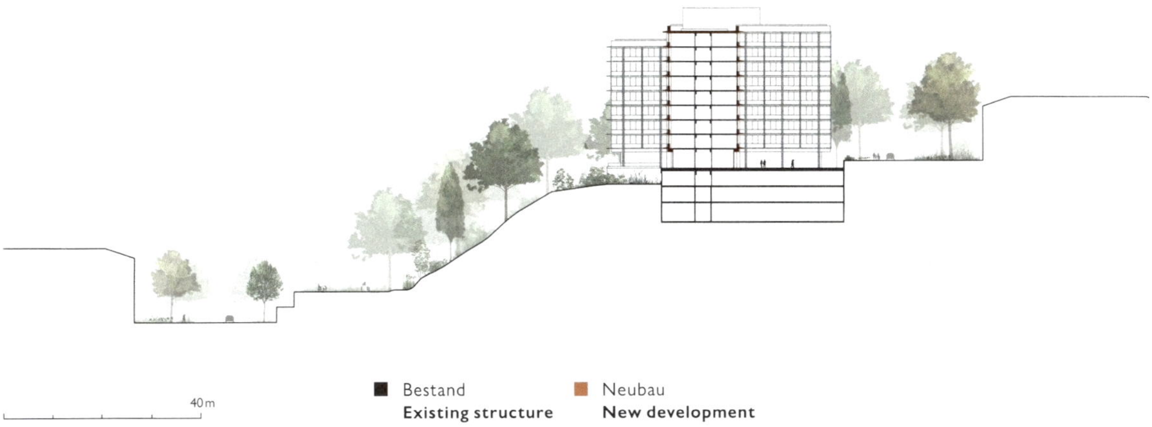
40 m
Bestand
Existing structure
Neubau
New development

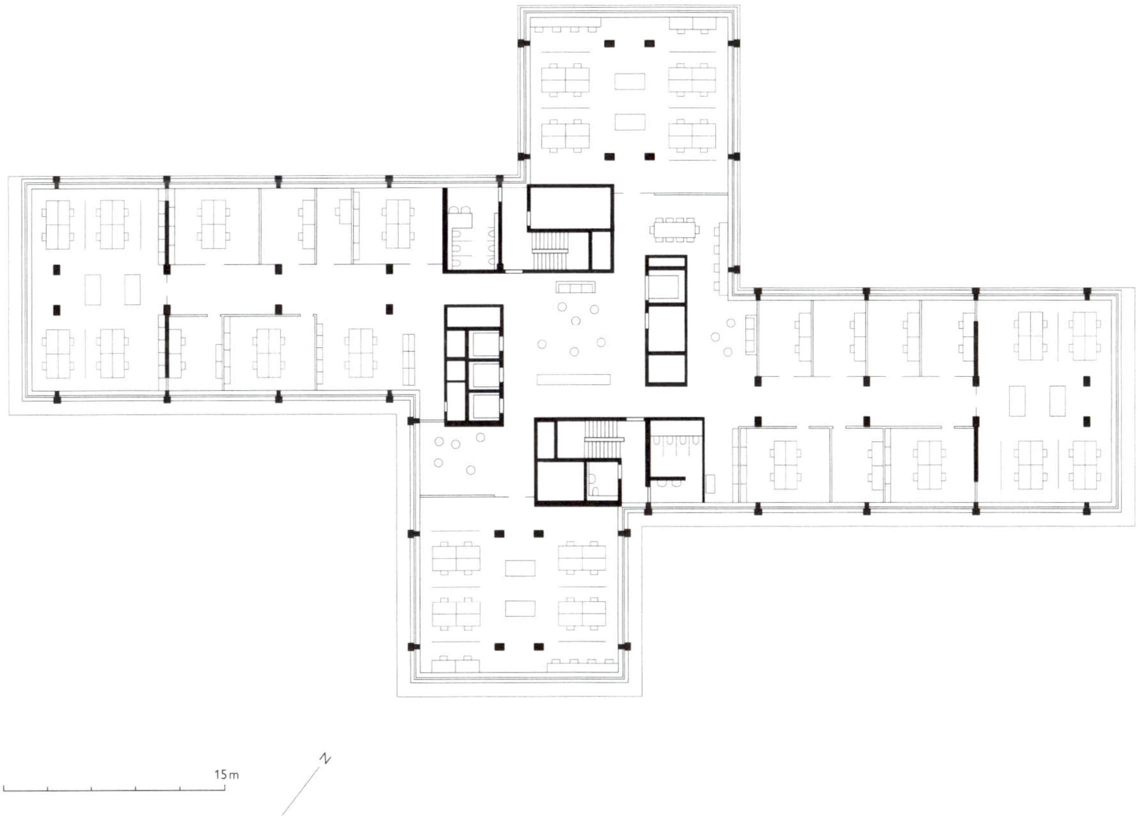
15 m
N

LOW TECH – LOW BUDGET – LOW ENERGY VERWALTUNGSGEBÄUDE, ITTIGEN

Auf einem ehemaligen Industriegelände bilden drei Neubauten ein Ensemble, das 1500 Mitarbeitenden differenzierten Raum und dem Verwaltungsstandort eine gemeinsame Identität gibt. Im grössten Bau erstreckt sich das Atrium über die gesamte Gebäudehöhe und bildet mit seinen Gemeinschaftsbereichen, Verwaltungsräumen und der Gastronomie die innere Adresse und den Treffpunkt aller Häuser. Zugleich ist es klimatischer Puffer und raumeffiziente Erschliessung des betreffenden Baukörpers.

Offene Grundrisse und ein einfaches statisches Konzept ermöglichen in allen drei Gebäuden verschiedenste Arbeitsformen. Die Bauweise gestattet eine höchst effiziente Flächennutzung und ein Maximum an Flexibilität – im Alltag wie auch bei grundlegenden Veränderungen der Nutzungsbedürfnisse. Die Häuser kommen mit wenig Technik aus und setzen auf natürliche Belüftung, Nachtauskühlung und Bauteilkühlung mit eigenem Quellwasser. Gemeinsam ist den Dreien auch ihre Hülle: eine nachhaltige Holzfassade aus Lamellen mit Tiefenwirkung. Das Bild wandelt sich mit der Perspektive des Betrachters.

Innovativer Holzbau, einfache Konstruktionen und Materialien, modulare Bauteile und eine reduzierte Haustechnik ermöglichen ein wirtschaftliches Ensemble mit niedrigen Betriebskosten und einer reichhaltigen Atmosphäre.

LOW TECH – LOW BUDGET – LOW ENERGY ADMINISTRATIVE BUILDING, ITTIGEN

On a former industrial estate, three new buildings form an ensemble, providing differentiated space for 1,500 employees and a common identity for the administrative quarter. Inside the largest volume, the atrium stretches over the entire building height and, with common areas, administrative spaces and catering facilities, forms the inner address and meeting point of all the buildings. At the same time, it offers a climatic buffer and spatially efficient access for the respective volumes.

Open floor plans and a simple load-bearing concept enable a wide range of working methods in all three buildings. The construction method allows the highly efficient use of space and maximum flexibility – in everyday life and also in the case of fundamental changes in user requirements. The buildings require only a few technical systems and focus on natural ventilation, night cooling and building-element cooling with its own well water. The three buildings also have the same envelope: a sustainable wooden façade made of lamellae with a three-dimensional effect. The image changes with the viewer's perspective.

Innovative wooden building, simple constructions and materials, modular building elements and reduced building technology ensure an economic ensemble with low operative costs and an abundant atmosphere.

Wettbewerb: 1997, 1. Rang
Realisierung: 2004–2006
Bauherrschaft: Bundesamt für Bauten und Logistik (BBL)

Competition: 1997, 1st Place
Construction: 2004–2006
Client: Bundesamt für Bauten und Logistik (BBL)

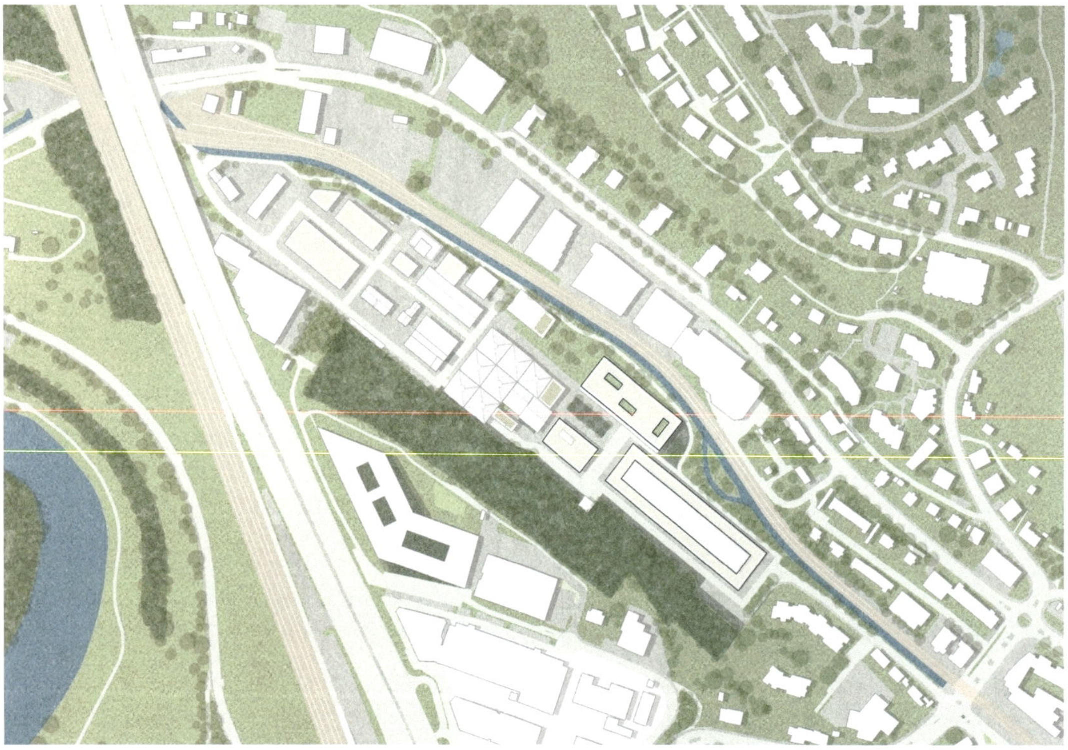

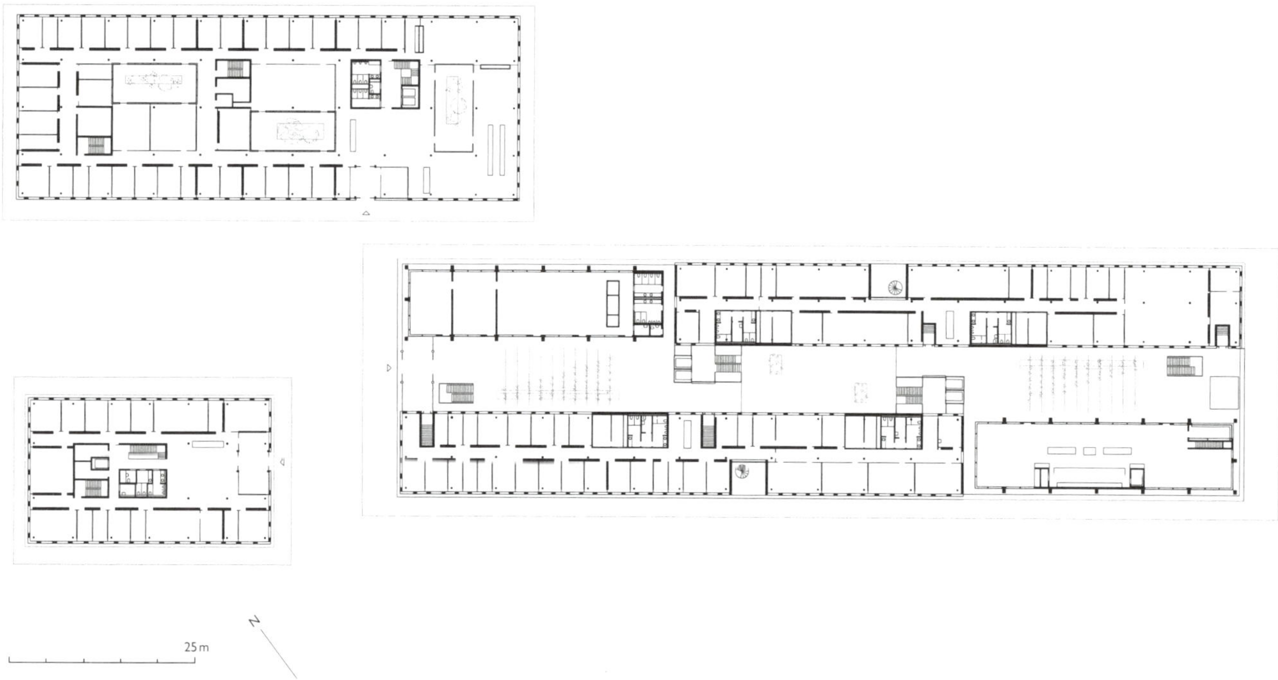
25 m
N

15 m

EINE SCHULE FÜRS QUARTIER UND FÜR DIE ZUKUNFT VOLKSSCHULE WEISSENBÜHL, BERN

A SCHOOL FOR THE NEIGHBOURHOOD AND THE FUTURE VOLKSSCHULE WEISSENBÜHL, BERN

Die Analyse des natürlichen und sozialräumlichen Umfelds der neuen Schule führte GWJ zu einem Gegenvorschlag zur Machbarkeitsstudie: Der Entwurf stellt die Qualitäten des parkartigen Freiraums zwischen Wald und Quartier in den Mittelpunkt und die Schule als dreiflügeliges Pavillonensemble leicht peripher in den Park. Sie profitiert so von den Qualitäten der «Gumere-Matte» und dem alten Baumbestand, für das Quartier bleibt das Areal als öffentlicher Raum nutzbar. Neue Freiraumtypen erweitern bestehende Freiraumqualitäten, schlecht nutzbare Orte werden in Wert gesetzt, etwa mit Sportanlagen entlang der Bahnlinie.

Adaptierbarkeit, Orientierung und kurze Wege sind zentrale Grundsätze der Pavillonarchitektur. Jeder Baukörper bietet flexible Lerncluster, organisiert werden sie über die verbindende Halle. Halle und Cluster sind räumlich veränderbar, die Balance zwischen Offenheit und Geschlossenheit lässt sich nach Bedarf anpassen. Verschiedene Möglichkeiten der Aneignung ermöglichen zeitgemässes, selbstorganisiertes Lernen, Gemeinschaft und Rückzug – für Lernende wie auch für Lehrende.

Die Konstruktion in Holzbauweise mit Lehmelementen und Lowtech-Gebäudetechnik setzt beim Klima und bei der Zirkularität neue Massstäbe für Bern. Mit dem vorgesehenen Standard SNBS Gold soll die Schule als Vorbild für zukünftige Bauvorhaben dienen.

The analysis of the natural and socio-spatial environment of the new school led GWJ to an alternative to the feasibility study: the design focused on the qualities of the park-like open space between the forest and the neighbourhood, placing the school as a three-winged pavilion ensemble in a slightly peripheral position in the park. It therefore benefits from the qualities of the "Gumere-Matte" and its old trees, while the area remains available as a public space for the neighbourhood. New types of open space supplement the existing qualities of the outdoor areas, thereby enhancing places that were difficult to use, for example through sports facilities along the railway line.

Adaptability, orientation and short distances are central guiding principles of the pavilion architecture. Each building offers flexible learning clusters, which are organised around a connecting hall. The hall and clusters can be spatially adjusted and the balance between open and closed spaces may be adapted as required. Diverse ranges of opportunities for appropriation enable contemporary and self-organised learning, community and retreat – for students and teachers.

The wooden construction with clay building elements and low-tech systems sets new standards in Bern with respect to climate sustainability and circular economy. With the intended SNBS Gold Standard, the school aims to serve as a model for future construction projects.

Offener Wettbewerb: 2022, 1. Rang
Realisierung: 2025–2028
Bauherrschaft: Stadt Bern
Kooperation:
GWJ Architektur AG, Bern
Chaves Biedermann GmbH, Basel

Open competition: 2022, 1st Place
Construction: 2025–2028
Client: City of Bern
Cooperation:
GWJ Architektur AG, Bern
Chaves Biedermann GmbH, Basel

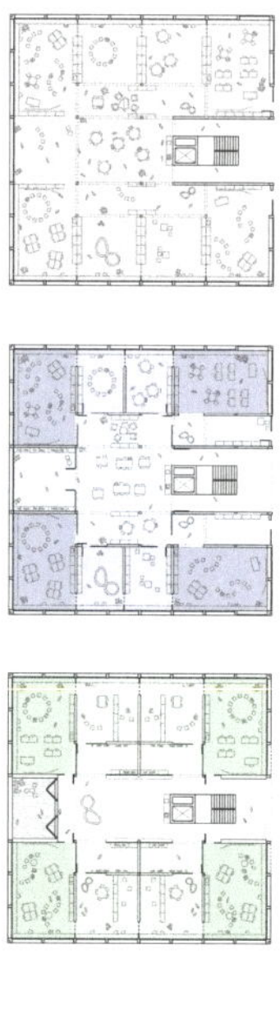

Offene Bildungslandschaft, Atelier / Ganztagesschule / Basisstufe
Open educational landscape, studio / All-day school / Primary level

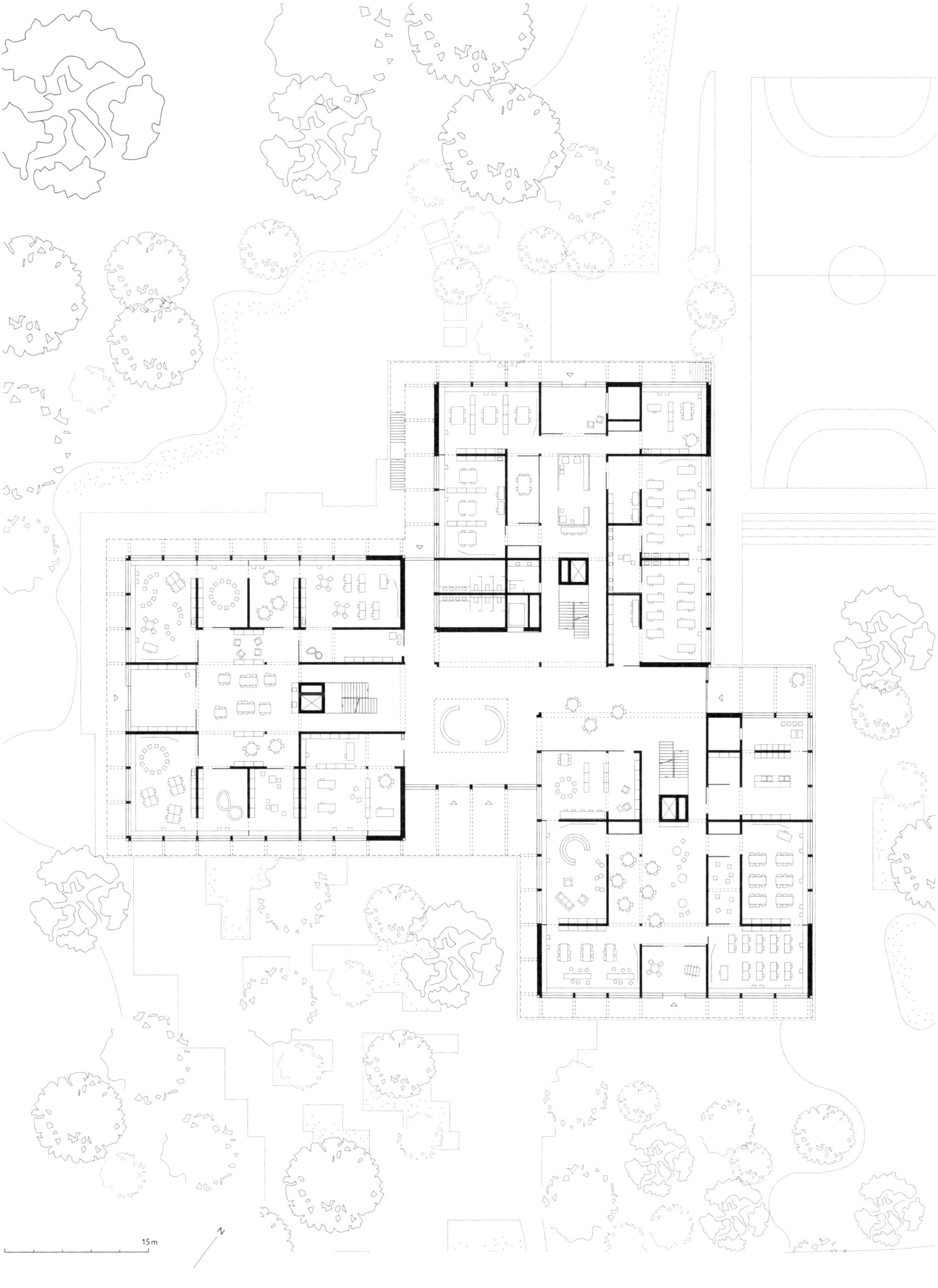
15m
N

LÖSUNGEN FÜR BEGRENZTEN HORIZONTALEN RAUM SCHULHAUS WALKA, ZERMATT

SOLUTIONS FOR LIMITED HORIZONTAL SPACE WALKA SCHOOL, ZERMATT

Im Bergdorf Zermatt ist das Bauen auf begrenztem Raum eine Notwendigkeit. Die extreme Topografie als Teil der Lösung zu verstehen und dabei das alte Schulhausensemble und die lokale Bautradition zum Vorbild zu nehmen, brachte den Wettbewerbserfolg.

Drei ineinander verschobene Baukörper fügen sich gestaffelt in den steilen Hang ein, integrieren sich in die dörflichen Strukturen auf der einen Seite und die landschaftlichen Gegebenheiten auf der anderen: Die neuen Pausenräume auf der Hangseite bieten beeindruckende Blicke auf das Matterhorn; an den gewachsenen Fels der unmittelbaren Umgebung schliesst der gebaute Raum klar und selbstverständlich an; und das grosszügige, verbindende Atrium über fünf Stockwerke ist direkte Antwort auf die extreme Hanglage.

Das Atrium ist der Dreh- und Angelpunkt der «niww Walka». Es dient als Eingangshalle, Pausen- und Aufenthaltsraum, von hier aus verteilen sich die Menschen und das Tageslicht in alle Teile des Schulhauses. Je nach Anlass macht das Atrium den Lernort zudem zum Treffpunkt für Eltern und die Dorfbevölkerung. Auch aus ortsbaulicher Sicht ist es der Kern der Lösung: Von innen betrachtet verbindet es die drei Baukörper und sorgt für Grosszügigkeit, von aussen lässt es ihnen ihre Eigenständigkeit und fügt sie in den dörflichen Massstab ein.

In the mountain village of Zermatt, building in limited space is imperative. Understanding the extreme topography as part of the solution and using the old schoolhouse ensemble and the local building tradition as inspiration led to competition success.

Three interconnected volumes merge into the steep slope in a staggered manner, integrating themselves into the village structures on one side and the landscape on the other. Impressive views of the Matterhorn can be enjoyed from the new lounge areas located on the slope side. The architectural space is directly and naturally connected to the rocky landscape of the immediate surroundings; the spacious, unifying atrium over five storeys is a direct response to the dramatic hillside location.

The atrium is the hub of the "niww Walka". It serves as an entrance hall, lounge area and gathering space, from where people spread out and daylight floods into all parts of the school building. The atrium also transforms the school into a meeting place for parents and the local community, depending on the occasion. It is also the key to the solution from an urban perspective: from the inside, it connects the three volumes and ensures spaciousness, while from the outside it gives them independence and blends them into the village scale.

Offener Wettbewerb: 2016, 1. Rang
Realisierung: 2021–2025
Bauherrschaft: Einwohnergemeinde EWG, Zermatt
Kooperation:
GWJ Architektur AG, Bern
Éxtra AG, Bern

Open competition: 2016, 1st Place
Construction: 2021–2025
Client: Einwohnergemeinde EWG, Zermatt
Cooperation:
GWJ Architektur AG, Bern
Éxtra AG, Bern

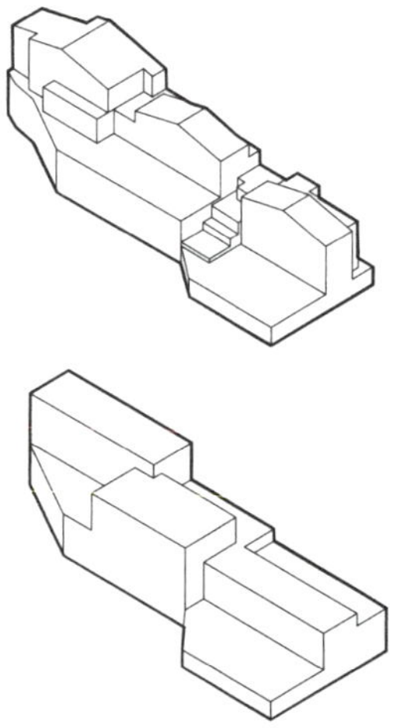

Die Typologie des Neubaus lehnt sich an das ehemalige Gebäude an.
The typology of the new building is inspired by its predecessor.

VILLA
TAUGWALDER
ALPINE GROUP
TREUHAND · FINANZEN · LIEGENSCHAFTEN
5m

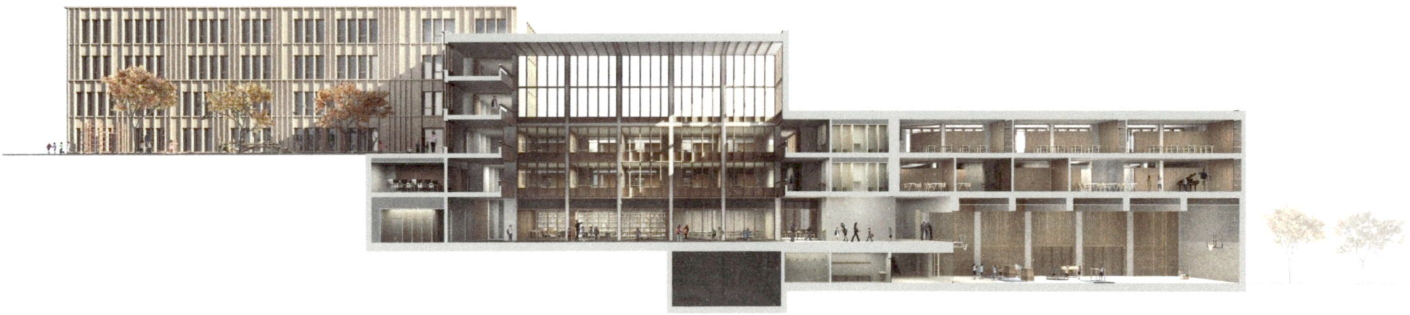

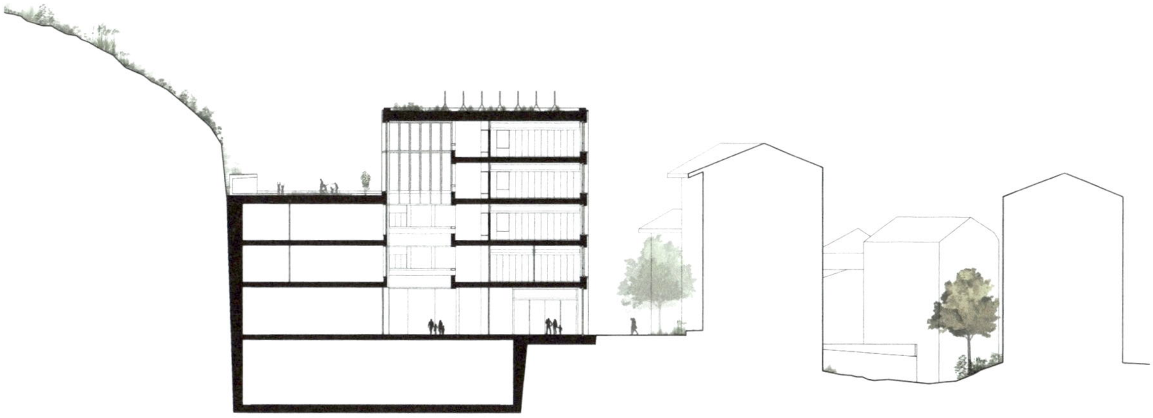

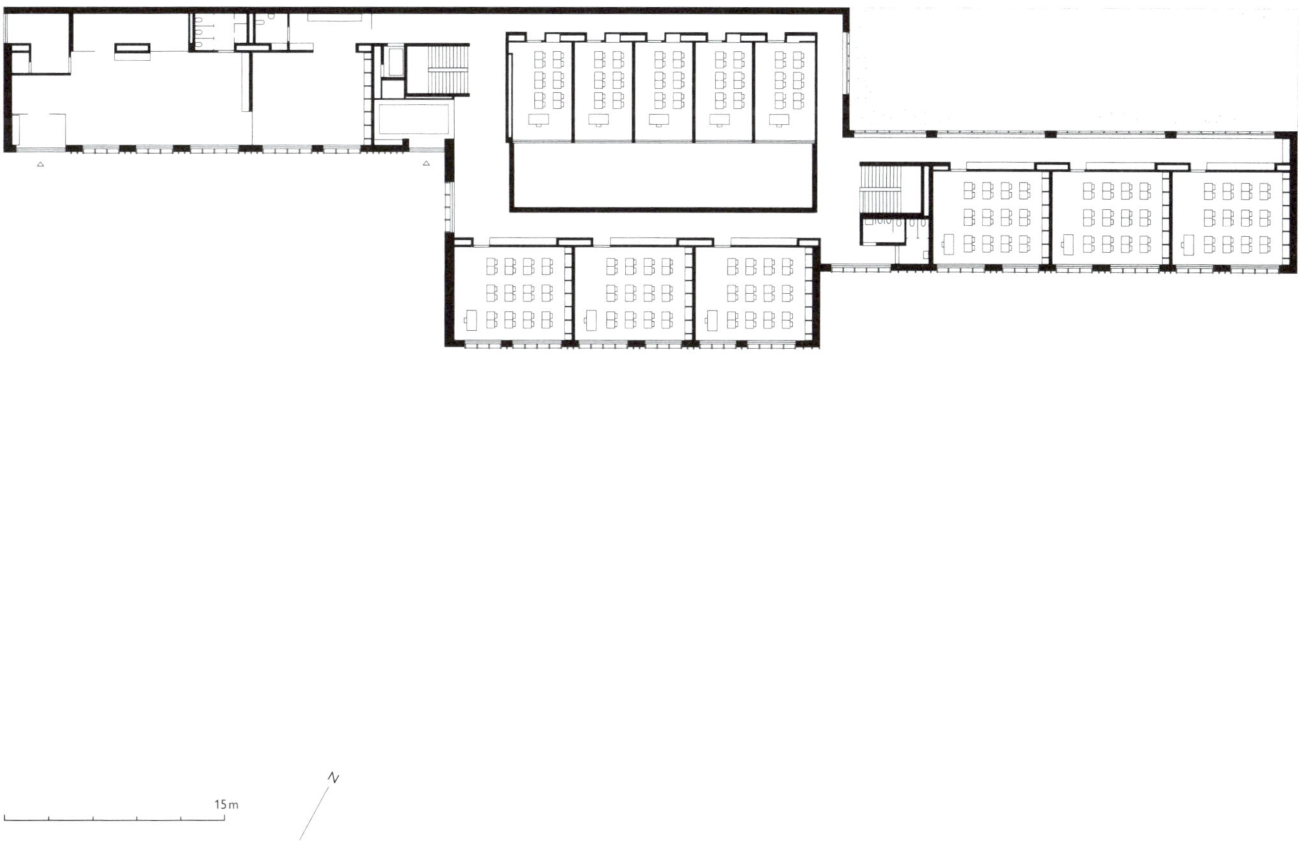
15m
N

LERNENDE STADT – LEBENDE STADT
BELL-AREAL, KRIENS

LEARNING CITY – LIVELY CITY
BELL-AREAL, KRIENS

Das Bell-Areal ist ein strategisches Entwicklungsgebiet inmitten von Kriens. Durch seine Transformation wird das introvertierte historische Industrieareal Teil der Stadt. Lage, Struktur und bauliche Geschichte bieten die seltene Chance, ein Nutzungsspektrum zu entwickeln, das über den klassischen Mix von Wohnen und Dienstleistung hinausgeht. Das städtebauliche Konzept schafft einen dynamischen Stadtraum für verschiedenste Interessengruppen.

Die historische Industriehalle C wird, auf Stützen und Dach reduziert, zum freiräumlichen Quartierzentrum. Plätze, Höfe, Wege, Gassen und Grünflächen bilden ein durchlässiges Freiraumnetz, das im Zusammenspiel mit den Gebäudenutzungen unterschiedliche Milieus und Atmosphären anbietet. Der Freiraum verbindet den neuen Stadtteil mit seiner städtischen Nachbarschaft.

Wo Neues und Bestehendes sich vermengen und sich sozialräumliche Dynamik entwickelt, lebt die Stadt. Wichtige Keimzellen solch einer gesunden Stadtentwicklung sind die räumlichen Übergänge. In der neuen Dichte des Bell-Areals balancieren Schwellenräume die Abstufungen von Öffentlichkeit und Privatheit fein aus. Aus der Logik des gewachsenen Areals entsteht ein zukunftsweisender Stadtraum von grosser funktionaler Vielfalt.

The Bell-Areal is a strategic development area at the centre of Kriens. Its transformation allows the introverted industrial site to become part of the city fabric. Its location, structure and architectural history offer an exceptional opportunity to develop a range of uses that goes beyond the classic mix of living and commercial services. The urban planning concept achieves a dynamic urban space for a diverse group of stakeholders.

Reduced to its columns and roof, the historical industrial Hall C becomes an outdoor neighbourhood centre. Squares, courtyards, paths, alleyways and green spaces create a permeable network of open areas that offer different environments and atmospheres, interplaying with the various building uses. The public space connects the new district to its urban surroundings.

Wherever new and existing elements come together and socio-spatial dynamics develop, the city comes alive. Spatial transitions are important factors in such healthy urban developments. In the Bell-Areal's new density, threshold spaces finely balance the gradations between public and private. A forward-looking urban space of great functional diversity is created from the underlying logic of the historically developed site.

Studienauftrag: 2021, 1 Rang
Bauherrschaft: Logis Suisse AG, Baden
Steiner AG, Zürich
Kooperation:
GWJ Architektur AG, Bern
Güller Güller, Zürich
ORT AG, Zürich
Soziale Plastik, Bern

Contracted study: 2021, 1st Place
Client: Logis Suisse AG, Baden
Steiner AG, Zurich
Cooperation:
GWJ Architektur AG, Bern
Güller Güller, Zurich
ORT AG, Zurich
Soziale Plastik, Bern

WORK
SOMEONE
BE CREATIVE
A PLANE
TODAY'S THE DAY

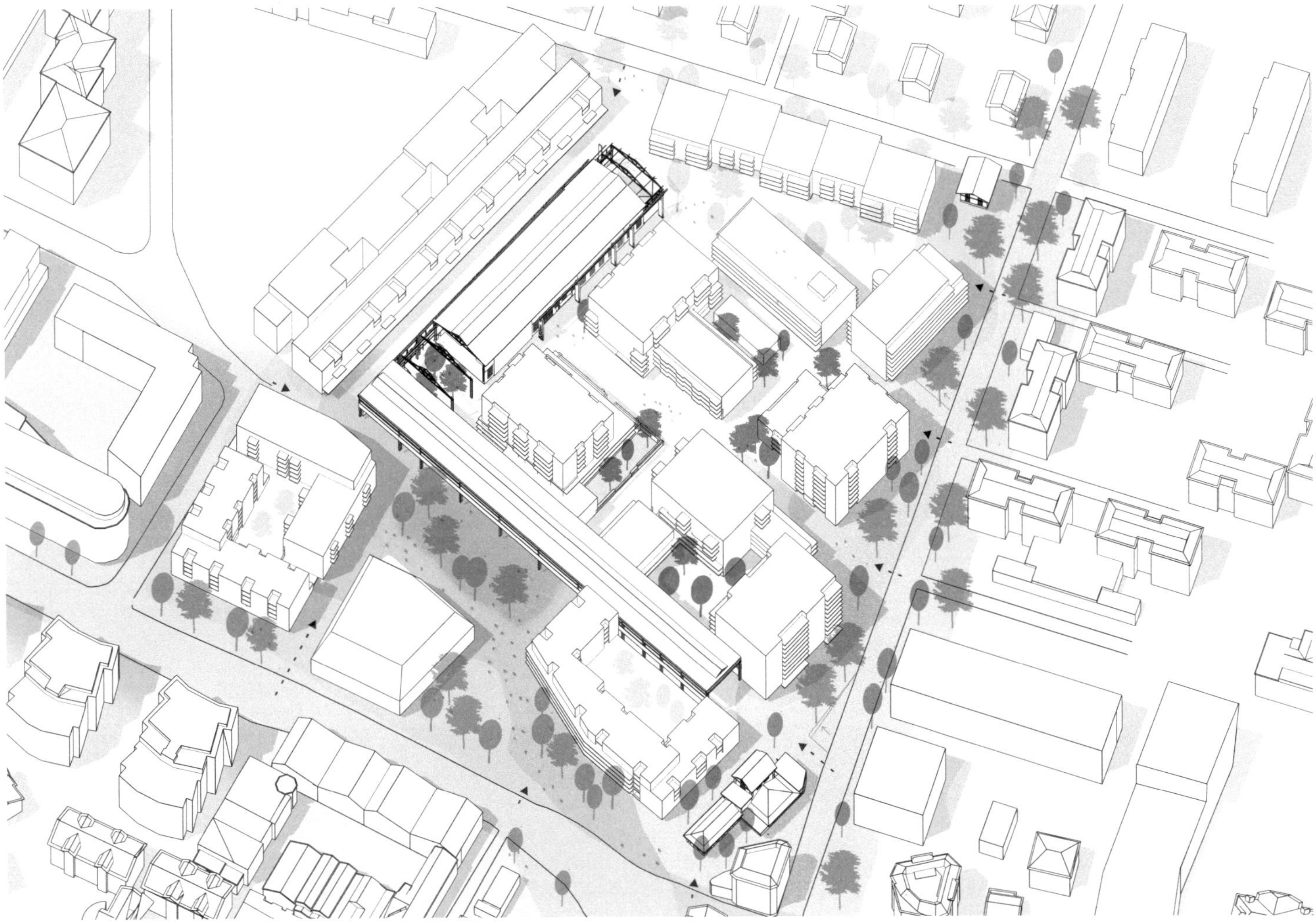

URBANER LEBENSRAUM ZWISCHEN GLEIS UND GRÜN WANKDORFFELDSTRASSE, BERN

URBAN HABITAT BETWEEN THE RAILWAY AND GREENERY WANKDORFFELDSTRASSE, BERN

Das lange, schmale Gewerbereal zwischen der Bahnstrecke und dem Nordquartier wird umgenutzt. Die Herausforderung: sieben Bauherrschaften mit unterschiedlichen Zeithorizonten, eine sehr hohe Zieldichte, die Integration in eine heterogene Nachbarschaft und gerade angesichts der Dichte hohe Anforderungen an soziale und bauliche Nachhaltigkeit.

Das neue Stadtstück vereint unterschiedliche Nutzungsmilieus, historische Strukturen bilden dabei die Ankerpunkte des Areals in seiner Geschichte. Freiraum und Sozialraum sind in der höheren Dichte essenziell. Nicht nur sorgen sie dank Schwammstadtprinzip für ein gutes Siedlungsklima: Plätze, Innenhöfe und öffentliche Grünflächen dienen neben Retention, Versickerung und Durchlüftung auch der sozialen und der ökologischen Vielfalt und Vernetzung. Selbst Gleis- und Strassenräume werden zu Lebensräumen für Flora, Fauna und in den Randbereichen für Menschen.

Das autoarme Quartier setzt auf kurze Wege, robuste Stadtbausteine, unterschiedliche Typologien und vernetzte Freiräume – und auf die lernende Planung: Sie ist als flexibler Entwicklungsprozess konzipiert. Bauabschnitte werden sukzessive umgesetzt, evaluiert und angepasst. Erfahrungen aus früheren Phasen werden laufend in die weitere Entwicklung zurückgespielt.

The long, narrow commercial area between the railway lines and the northern neighbourhood is being redeveloped. The challenge: seven clients with different timelines, a very high target density, integration into a heterogeneous neighbourhood and, especially in view of the density, considerable demands in terms of social and structural sustainability.

The new urban area combines different user milieus while historical structures define the anchor points of the area's development. Open and social spaces are essential in this higher density. Not only do they ensure a good urban climate thanks to the "Sponge City" principle, with squares, inner courtyards and public green spaces enabling rainwater retention, seepage and air circulation, but social and ecological diversity and connectivity are also achieved. Even railway tracks and streets become habitats for flora, fauna and, in peripheral areas, people.

The low car traffic district is characterised by short distances, robust urban building blocks, different typologies and interconnected open spaces – and by adaptive planning: it is designed as a flexible development process. Urban development phases are successively implemented, evaluated and adapted. Experiences from earlier stages are continuously incorporated into further development.

Ideenstudie: 2022, 1. Rang
Masterplan: 2024
Bauherrschaft: Baurechtnehmer:innnen
Areal «Wankdorffeldstrasse Bern»
Gebäudeversicherung Bern
AXA Investment Managers Schweiz AG
Genossenschaft Migros Aare
Halter AG
Alb. Wahlen AG
Kooperation:
GWJ Architektur AG, Bern
ASTOC AG, Köln
Jungheim GmbH, Bern
Samuel Métraux GmbH, Bern
Treibhaus AG, Hamburg
ORT AG, Zürich
Soziale Plastik, Bern

Concept study: 2022, 1st Place
Master plan: 2024
Client: Baurechtnehmer:innnen
Areal "Wankdorffeldstrasse Bern"
Gebäudeversicherung Bern
AXA Investment Managers Schweiz AG
Genossenschaft Migros Aare
Halter AG
Alb. Wahlen AG
Cooperation:
GWJ Architektur AG, Bern
ASTOC AG, Cologne
Jungheim GmbH, Bern
Samuel Métraux GmbH, Bern
Treibhaus AG, Hamburg
ORT AG, Zurich
Soziale Plastik, Bern

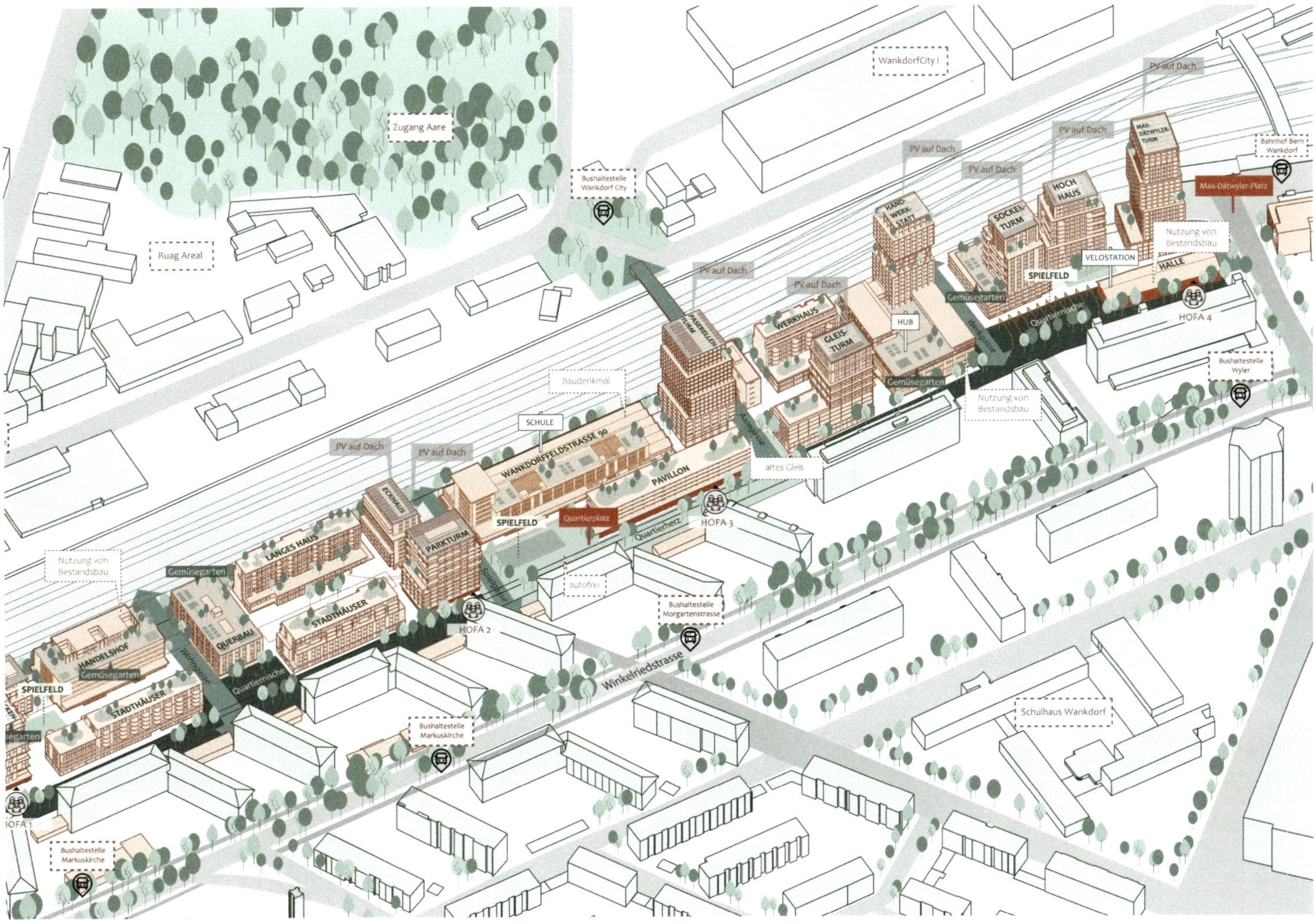

WankdorfCity I
Zugang Aare
Bushaltestelle Wankdorf City
Ruag Areal
PV auf Dach
Bahnhof Bern Wankdorf
Max-Dätwyler-Platz
MAX-DÄTWYLER-TURM
HOCH HAUS
SOCKEL-TURM
HAND-WERK-STATT
Nutzung von Bestandsbau
VELOSTATION
HALLE
SPIELFELD
Gemüsegarten
HOFA 4
Quartiermische
WERKHAUS
GLEIS-TURM
HUB
Bushaltestelle Wyler
Baudenkmal
SCHULE
WANKDORFFELDSTRASSE 90
PAVILLON
altes Gleis
HOFA 3
Quartierplatz
Quartierherz
ECKHAUS
PARKTURM
LANGES HAUS
autofrei
Bushaltestelle Morgartenstrasse
HOFA 2
STADTHÄUSER
QUERBAU
HANDELSHOF
Winkelriedstrasse
Bushaltestelle Markuskirche
HOFA 1
Schulhaus Wankdorf

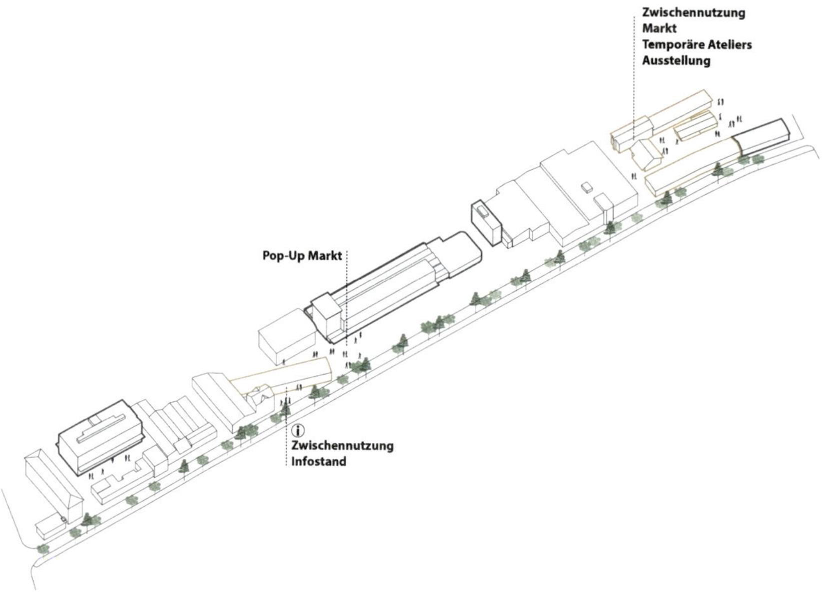

Transformationsprozess
Transformation process

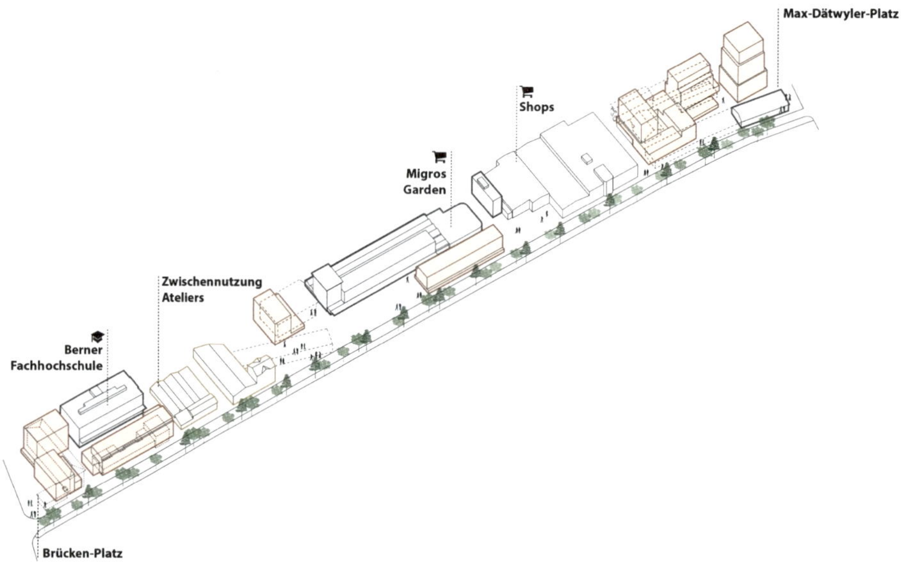

Weiternutzen, umnutzen, verdichten
Continued use, conversion, densification

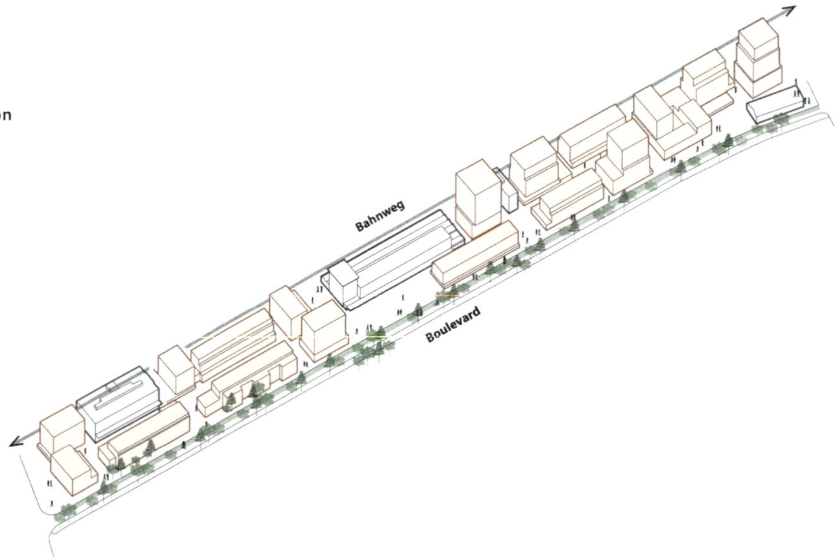

Weiterentwickeln
Further development

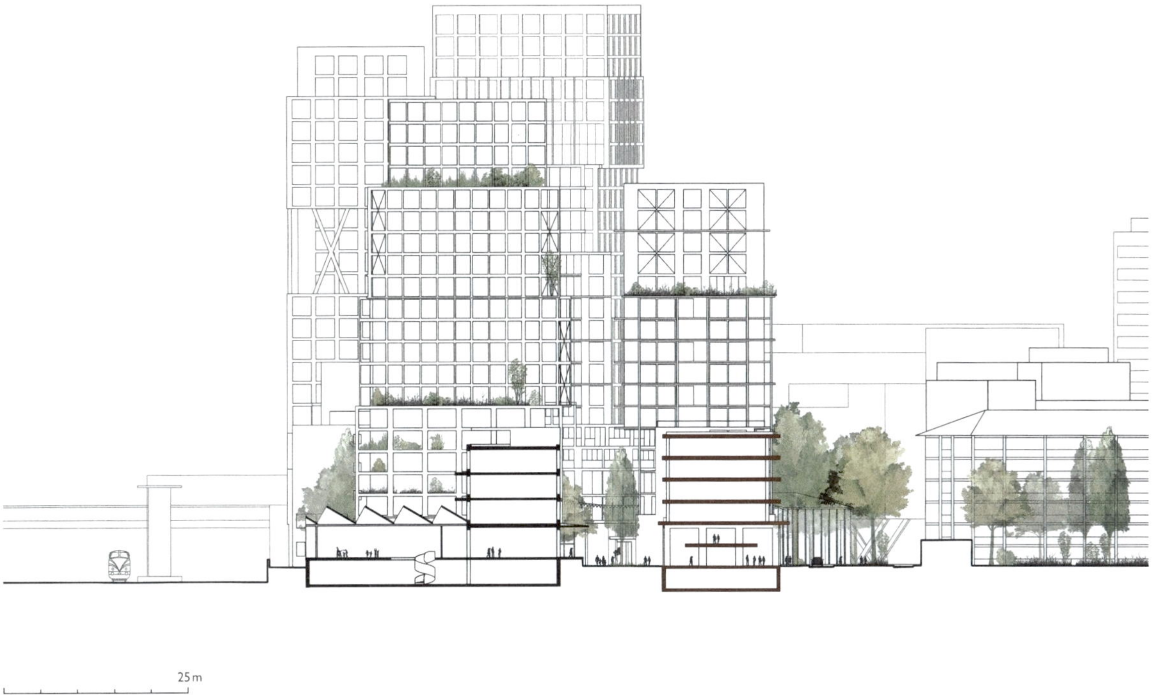
25 m

Schule

RAUM FÜR HEILUNG
KINDER- UND JUGENDPSYCHIATRIE (UPD), BERN

**SPACE FOR HEALING
CHILDREN'S AND ADOLESCENT PSYCHIATRIC CENTRE (UPD), BERN**

Der Campus der Universitären Psychiatrischen Dienste ist in einem denkmalgeschützten Gebäudeensemble innerhalb eines weitläufigen Parks untergebracht. Jeder bauliche Entwicklungsschritt der UPD und damit jedes Gebäude steht für sich und seine Entstehungszeit. Der Neubau der Kinder- und Jugendpsychiatrie KJP folgt dieser Logik in seiner städtebaulichen Setzung und architektonischen Haltung.

Die KJP ist Therapieort, aber auch Lebens- und Alltagsraum für die Jugendlichen – im Spannungsfeld zwischen Ausnahmesituation und temporärer Normalität. Zwei Wohntrakte und ein Kliniktrakt machen die komplexen Raumanforderungen überschaubar und eine klare Adressierung möglich. Zwischen den freigestellten Baukörpern liegt der «Ort der Begegnung», das Rückgrat der Anlage.

Die feine Abstufung von Gemeinschaft zu Privatheit ist vom Freiraum bis zur Architektur das durchgängige Thema. Auch die Wohngruppen folgen diesem Prinzip. Leitmotiv ist hier das Bild der Wohngemeinschaft. Mehrere Doppelzimmer gruppieren sich um einen Gemeinschaftsbereich. Der Wohn- und Essbereich ist zentral, offen und kommunikativ konzipiert, der ruhigere Rückzugsbereich zum Atrium orientiert.

Die Gestaltung legt Wert auf eine kindgerechte Umsetzung des Programms, entsprechende Dimensionen und feingliedrige Strukturen. Dies und die sichtbare, einladende Holzbauarchitektur sorgen für ein wohltuendes Umfeld.

The campus of the University Psychiatric Services is a historical building ensemble surrounded by an ample park. Each architectural development for the UPD and therefore each building is autonomous and represents its period. The new building of the Child and Adolescent Psychiatry (KJP) follows this logic in its urban setting and architectural approach.

The KJP is a place of therapy, but also a living and everyday space for young people – somewhere between an exceptional situation and temporary normality. Two residential wings and a clinic wing make the complex spatial requirements easy to understand, forming a clear address. Between the free-standing buildings, the "encounter area" forms the backbone of the facility.

The subtle transition from community to privacy is the consistent principle throughout, from the outdoor space to the architecture. The residential units also follow this principle. Their leitmotif is the idea of cohabitation. Several double rooms are arranged around a common area. The living and dining spaces are designed to be central, open and welcoming, while the quieter retreat zones are orientated towards the atrium.

The design focuses on a child-friendly approach to the programme, suitable scales and delicate structures. This and the visible, warm wooden architecture create a pleasant environment.

Selektiver Studienauftrag: 2023, 1. Rang
Bauherrschaft: Universitäre Psychiatrische Dienste Bern (UPD)
Kooperation:
GWJ Architektur AG, Bern
CO. Architekten AG, Bern
Chaves Biedermann GmbH, Basel

**Invitation contracted study: 2023, 1st Place
Client: Universitäre Psychiatrische Dienste Bern (UPD)
Cooperation:
GWJ Architektur AG, Bern
CO. Architekten AG, Bern
Chaves Biedermann GmbH, Basel**

HAUS 2

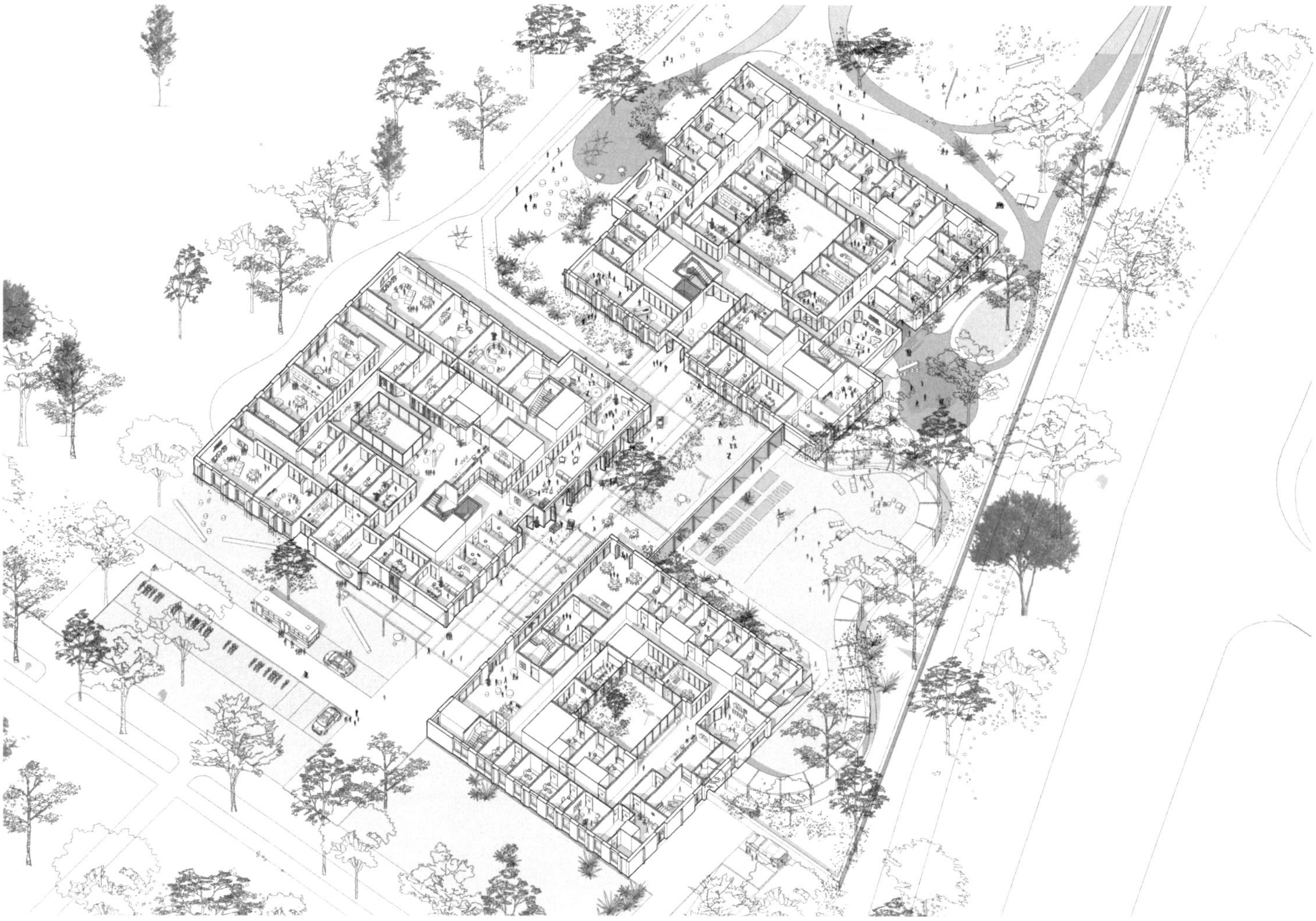

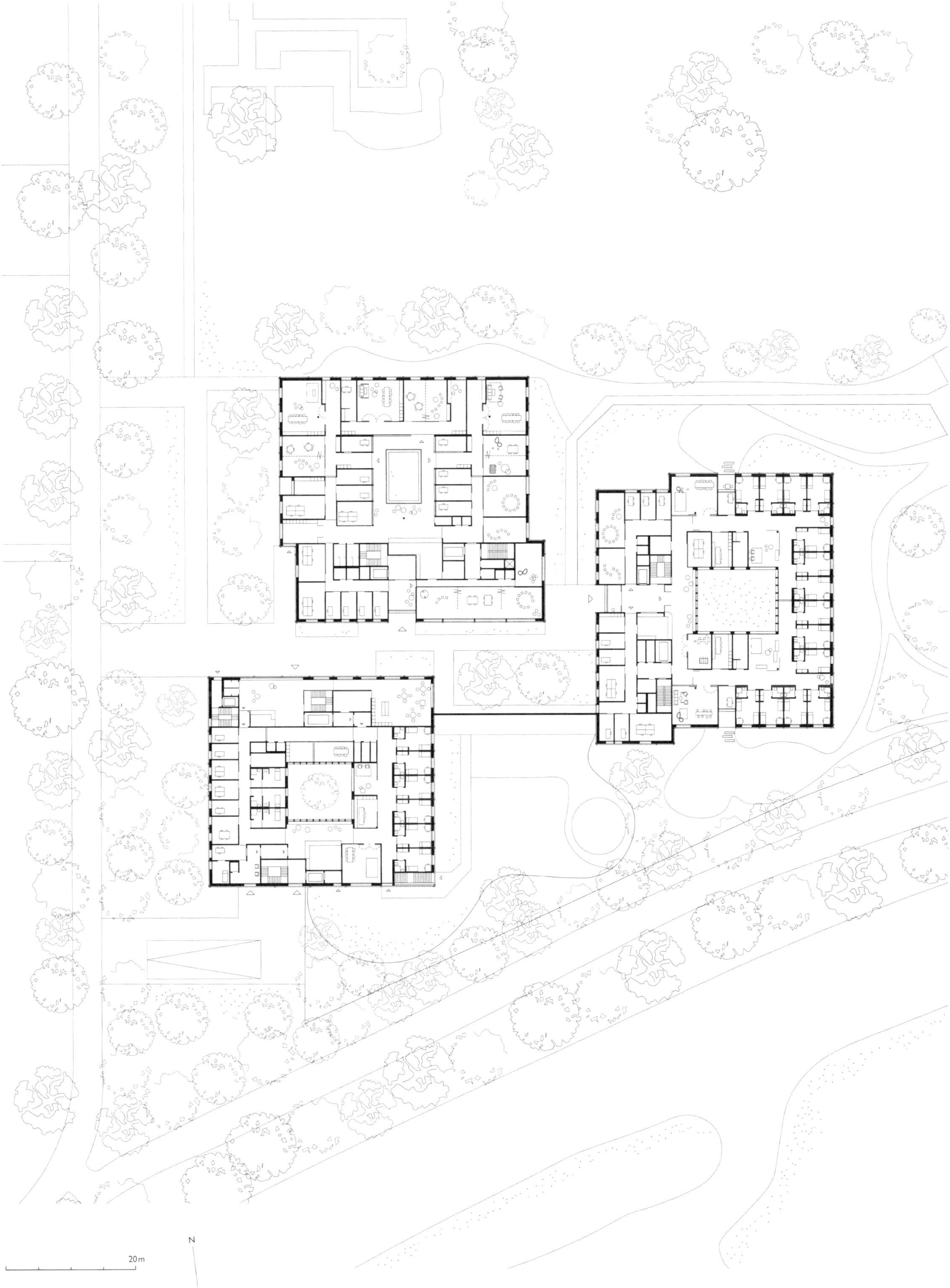
20 m
N

ZWISCHEN HERMETIK UND OFFENHEIT
FORSCHUNGS- UND AUSBILDUNGS-ZENTRUM, UNIVERSITÄT, BERN

Zur Stärkung des Medizinalstandorts Bern wird die Medizinische Fakultät der Universität ausgebaut, ihre Institute werden auf dem Inselareal konzentriert. Das Synergiepotenzial dieser Nähe gilt es auch über die Architektur nutzbar zu machen. Die Anforderungen sind ungewöhnlich und gegensätzlich: Die Forschung erfordert geschützte Räume, die Lehre offenen Austausch, und multifunktionale Veranstaltungsflächen sollen Begegnungen anregen, den Alltag attraktiver und besondere Anlässe möglich machen.

Eine klare innere Gebäudeorganisation ist die Basis für eine hohe Funktionalität und Anpassungsfähigkeit. Die offene Arbeits- und Bildungslandschaft orientiert sich auf ganzer Gebäudelänge zur Strasse. Die hermetisch abgeschlossene Laborschicht mit zwei kompakten Erschliessungskernen liegt auf der Seite des Pocket Parks. Als Orte des Ankommens und des Austauschs dienen das offene Erdgeschoss und – auf allen Ebenen – die Mitte mit der markanten Wendeltreppe. Die verschiedenen Gebäudeteile unterscheiden sich auch in der Lebensdauer, was in der Gebäudekonzeption ebenfalls zu berücksichtigen ist.

Eine minimale Tragstruktur, ein strenges Ausbauraster und die Logik der Gebäudeorganisation ermöglichen den Spagat zwischen Modularität, klar getrennten Gebäudeschichten, gestaffelter Rückbaubarkeit und der Adaptierbarkeit der Räume von Forschungsgruppen oder ganzen Instituten. Konsequente Systemtrennung ermöglicht Reparatur, Sanierung und Demontage im Geist der Kreislaufwirtschaft.

BETWEEN HERMETIC CLOSURE AND OPENNESS
RESEARCH AND TRAINING CENTRE, UNIVERSITY, BERN

To strengthen Bern as a medical hub, the University's Faculty of Medicine is being expanded and its institutions are being centralised on the *Inselareal* campus. The synergy potential offered by this proximity needs to be maximised through the architecture. The project's requirements are unusual and contradictory: research facilities require protection, teaching areas require communication, and multifunctional event spaces are intended to foster interaction, making everyday life attractive and enabling special occasions.

A clear interior building organisation forms the basis for a high level of functionality and adaptability. The open working and educational landscape is orientated towards the street along the entire length of the building. The hermetically sealed laboratory section, with two compact access cores, is located on the pocket park side. The open ground floor and – on all levels – the central area with its characteristic spiral staircase provide arrival and meeting areas. Building components also differ in terms of their service life, which must be taken into account in the building design.

A minimal load-bearing structure, a strict construction grid and the building organisation logic enable a successful combination of modularity, clearly separated building layers, staggered demountability and the adaptability of rooms for research groups or entire institutes. Consistent system separation enables repair, renovation and dismantling in the spirit of the circular economy.

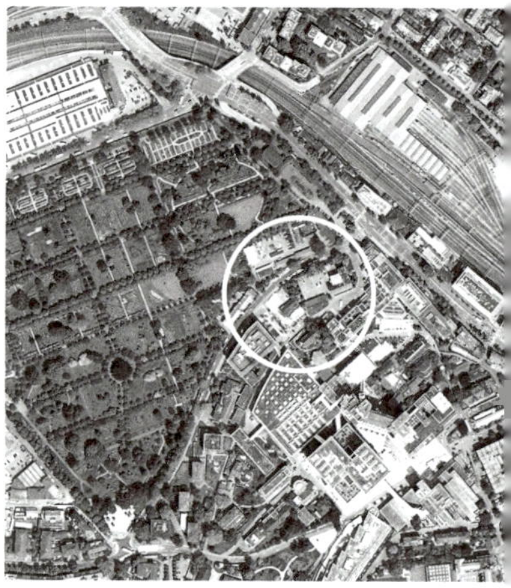

Projektwettbewerb: 2020, 1. Rang
Realisierung: 2024–2031
Bauherrschaft: Amt für Grundstücke und Gebäude des Kantons Bern AGG
Kooperation:
GWJ Architektur AG, Bern
IAAG Architekten AG, Bern
ASTOC Architects GmbH, Köln
Archipel Generalplanung AG, Bern

Project competition: 2020, 1st Place
Construction: 2024–2031
Client: Amt für Grundstücke und Gebäude des Kantons Bern AGG
Cooperation:
GWJ Architektur AG, Bern
IAAG Architekten AG, Bern
ASTOC Architects GmbH, Cologne
Archipel Generalplanung AG, Bern

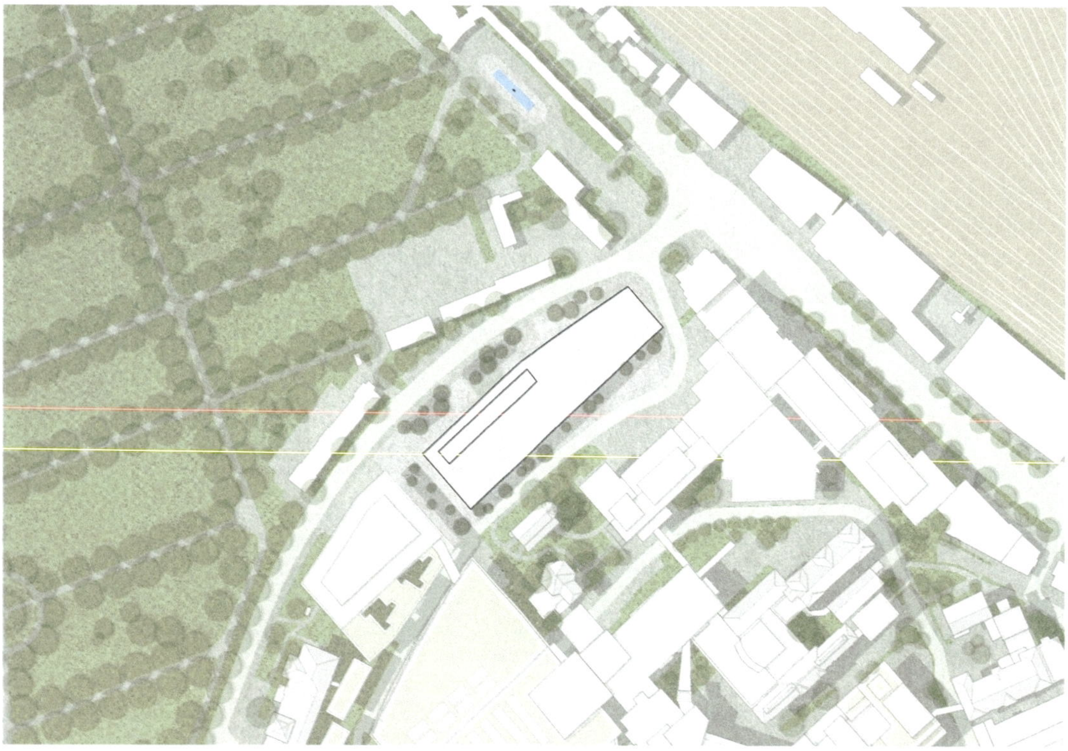

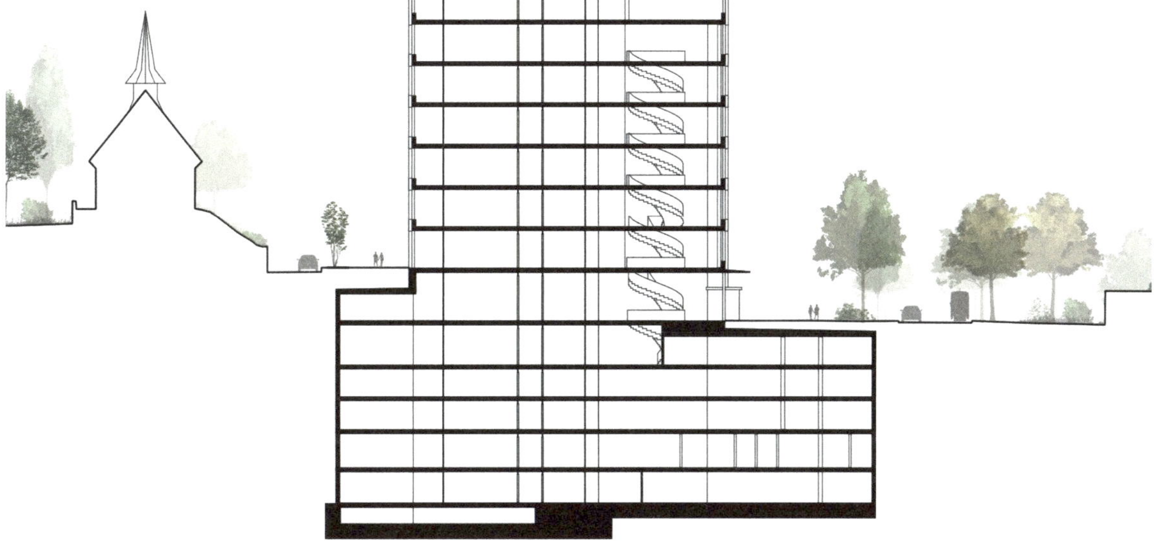

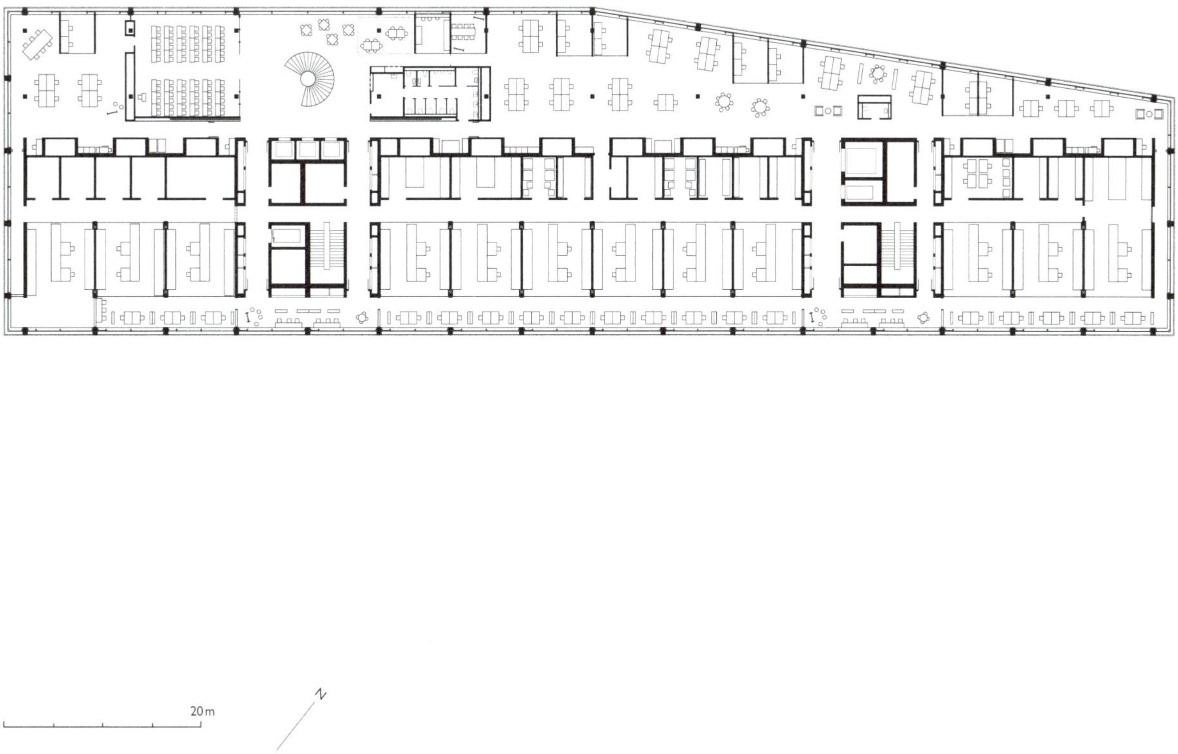

20 m
N

DIE GESUNDHEITS-STADT IN DER STADT
ANNA-SEILER-HAUS, INSELSPITAL, BERN

A HEALTH CITY WITHIN A CITY
ANNA-SEILER-HAUS, INSELSPITAL, BERN

Täglich finden sich hier 1600 Mitarbeitende und 1200 Patientinnen und Patienten ein, auf 82 000 Quadratmetern, in 3245 Räumen von 11 Kliniken und Instituten: Das Anna-Seiler-Haus ist das Hauptgebäude und mit 20 Stockwerken ein Orientierungspunkt des Berner Inselareals. Als erstes Spital in der Schweiz erfüllt es den Passivhausstandard Minergie-P-ECO.

Der Neubau bietet mit dem Konzept der gestapelten Stadt eine einfache Lösung für eine höchst komplexe Aufgabe: Im Sockel liegen die klinischen Einrichtungen, in den Türmen, mit Ruhe und Aussicht, die Bettenstationen. Das Plattformkonzept erleichtert dank der räumlichen Nähe der Kliniken und Institute die Arbeit und fördert durch kurze Wege Synergien. Es ermöglicht auch die nötige Privatheit in den Türmen. Zwischen die klinischen Bereiche und die Bettenstationen schiebt sich das Technikgeschoss. Seine Lage verkürzt Installationswege und gewährleistet Flexibilität.

Der Entwurf fasst das technisch und räumlich anspruchsvolle Innenleben des Gesundheitsbaus und seine unterschiedlichen Teile in eine schlichte Form und in eine unaufgeregte, hochwertige Fassade, was dem Inselareal wie auch der Stadt rundum gerecht wird. Innen ein menschlicher und effizienter Spitalbau, aussen ein Koloss von schlichter Anmut.

Bewährt hat sich die Arbeit ohne Totalunternehmer. Die Leitung von Planung, Ausführung und Realisierung lag bei der Planergemeinschaft Archipel (GWJ, IAAG, ASTOC und ab 2018 Archipel Generalplanung). Das Spital wurde termingerecht und im Rahmen des Budgets in Betrieb genommen.

Every day, 1,600 employees and 1,200 patients gather on a space of 82,000 square metres, in the 3,245 rooms of the 11 clinics and institutes. Anna-Seiler-Haus is the main building and, with 20 floors, a landmark on the Bern's Inselareal campus. It is the first hospital in Switzerland to fulfil the Minergie-P-ECO passive house standard.

With its concept of a stacked city, the new building offers a simple solution for a highly complex task: the clinical facilities are located in the base, while the wards are in the two towers, offering a peaceful and quiet atmosphere, with views of the city of Bern. The platform design facilitates workflows and promotes synergies through short distances, thanks to the close proximity to other clinics and institutes. It also provides the necessary privacy in the towers. The technical floor is located between the clinical areas and the wards. Its location shortens installation routes and ensures flexibility.

The design combines the technically and spatially sophisticated interior of the healthcare building and its various parts into a simple form with a calm, high-quality façade that fits in seamlessly with both the Inselareal campus and the city. A human and efficient hospital building on the inside, a colossus of simple appearance on the outside.

Working without a general contractor has proved helpful. The planning partnership Archipel (GWJ, IAAG, ASTOC and, from 2018, Archipel Generalplanung) was responsible for planning, implementation and construction. The hospital went into operative duty on time and within budget.

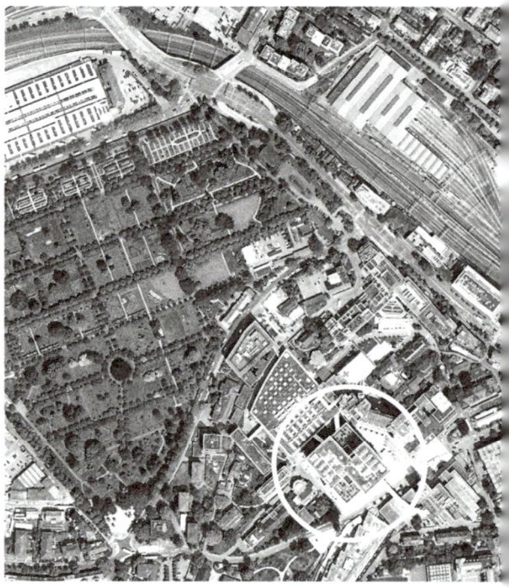

Projektwettbewerb: 2014, 1. Rang
Realisierung: 2017–2023
Bauherrschaft: Inselspital, Universitätsspital Bern
Kooperation:
GWJ Architektur AG, Bern
IAAG Architekten AG, Bern
ASTOC Architects, Köln
ab 2018: Archipel Generalplanung, Bern

Project competition: 2014, 1st Place
Construction: 2017–2023
Client: Inselspital, Universitätsspital Bern
Cooperation:
GWJ Architektur AG, Bern
IAAG Architekten AG, Bern
ASTOC Architects, Cologne
from 2018: Archipel Generalplanung, Bern

INSEL
INSEL

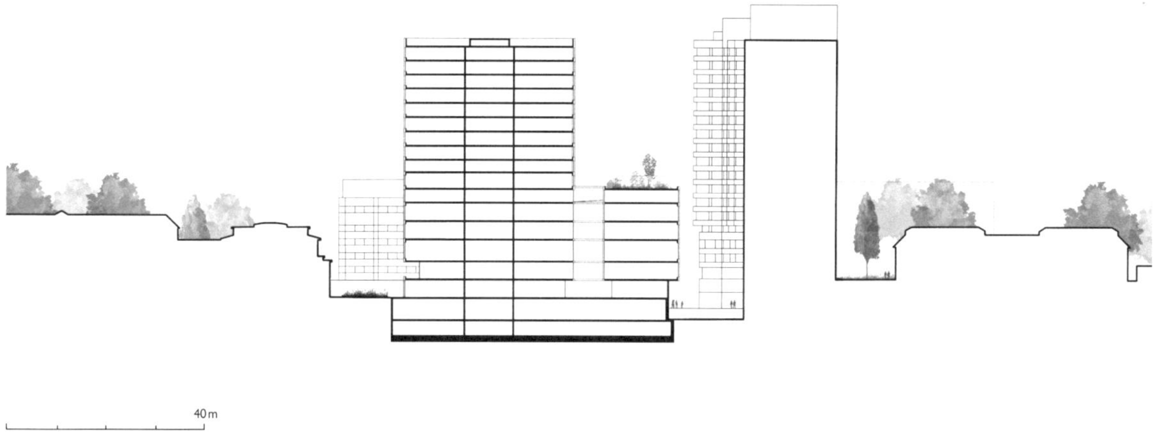
40 m

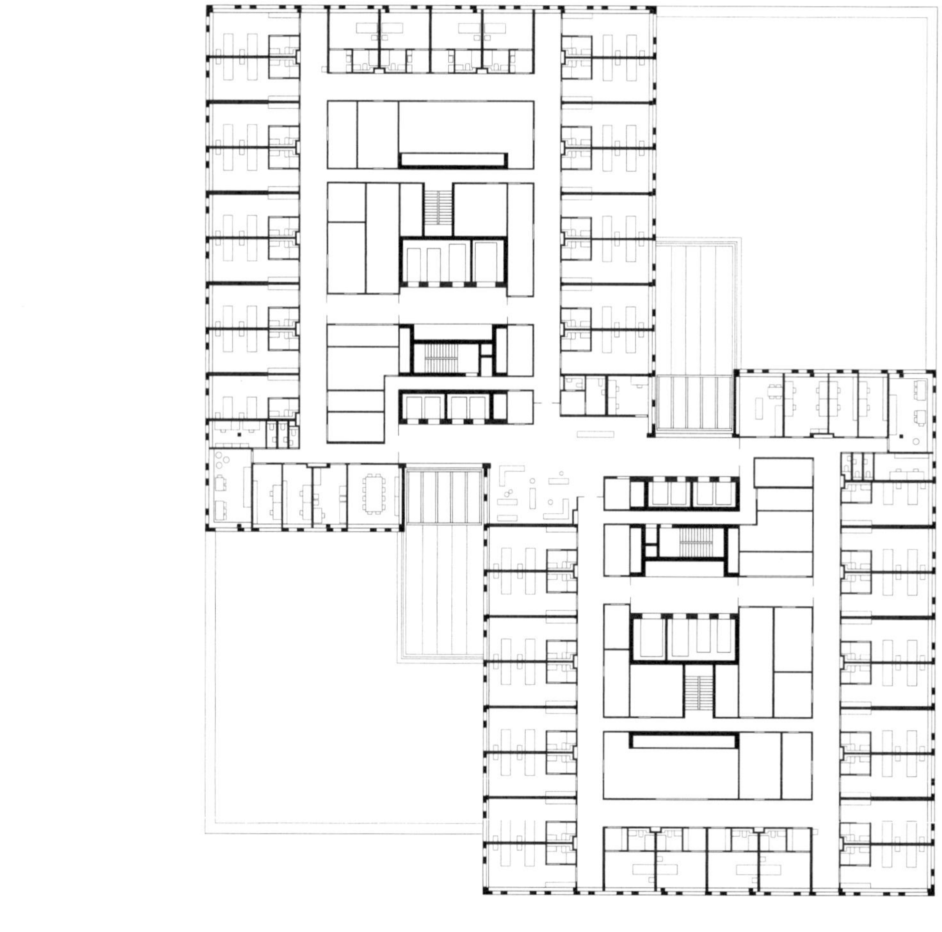
20 m
N

INSEL
INSEL
ZONE
Lausanne
Kante F

WERKVERZEICHNIS
Auswahl Bauten, Projekte und Wettbewerbe

1992 1 Internationaler Wettbewerb Neues Regierungsviertel Spreebogen, Berlin (3. Preis)
1998 2 Bürogebäude, Ittigen (Wettbewerb 1991, 1. Rang)
2003 3 Synchrotron Lichtquelle, Villigen (Studienauftrag 1996, 1. Rang)
2004 4 Masterplan Ban de Gasperich, Luxemburg
2006 Verwaltungsgebäude, Ittigen (Wettbewerb 1997, 1. Rang)
2007 5 Campus Careum, Zürich-Fluntern (Wettbewerb 2000, 1. Rang)
2010 6 Internationaler Wettbewerb Masterplan Inselareal, Bern (2. Rang)
2011 7 Transformation Alti Sagi, Innerberg
Entwicklungsstrategie Universitätsspital, Zürich
2013 Transformation Areal Gurtenbrauerei, Wabern (Arealentwicklung 2004, Studienauftrag 2008)
Entwicklungsstrategie Gemeinde Rubigen
2014 8 Testplanung AggloLac, Biel (2. Rang)
Denkmalgeschütztes Mehrfamilienhaus Gerberngasse, Bern
Entwicklungsstrategie Weiler Ried
2015 9 Modernisierung Bürogebäude Mobiliar, Bern
2016 Wettbewerb Gesamtsanierung Taubenhalde, Bern (1. Rang)
2017 10 Mehrfamilienhaus Lorrainestrasse, Bern
Wettbewerb Bubenberg Bahnhof Zugang, Bern
Studienauftrag Marktgasse, Bern
Testplanung Zentrumsentwicklung, Gümligen
2018 Studienauftrag van Baerle Areal, Münchenstein (1. Rang)
Wettbewerb Campus ZHAW, Winterthur (4. Rang)
2019 11 Projektentwicklung Demenzdorf, Wiedlisbach
Wettbewerb Viererfeld, Bern
Wettbewerb Schulcampus, Sion
Testplanung Gwattstrasse, Thun
Studienauftrag Wohngebäude Du Lac, Merligen
Studienauftrag Spühlirain, Schliern
12 Testplanung Dreieck Süd, Zollikofen (1. Rang)
Wettbewerb Hochhaus Lischenmoos, Gümligen (3. Rang)
13 Wettbewerb Kasernenareal, Zürich (2. Rang / 1. Preis)
Testplanung Zentrum Fünf-Egg, Muri (1. Rang)
2020 14 Wankdorf City II, Bern (Wettbewerb 2015, 1. Rang)
15 Wettbewerb Mehrfamilienhäuser Chirchbüel, Zumikon (1. Rang)
Wettbewerb Campus Platztor der Uni, St. Gallen (7. Rang)
Wettbewerb Anderes Wohnen, Zollikofen
2021 Huebergass und Stadtteilpark, Bern (Wettbewerb 2017, 1. Rang)
Wettbewerb Baubereich 04, Universitätsspital, Bern
16 Testplanung Saurer Werk Zwei, Arbon (1. Rang)
2022 17 Gangloff Areal, Bern
Wettbewerb Unterfeld Süd, Baar
2023 Anna-Seiler-Haus, Inselspital, Bern (Wettbewerb 2014, 1. Rang)
18 Füllerichstrasse, Gümligen (Wettbewerb 2018, 1. Rang)
19 Wettbewerb Kantonsschule, Stein (3. Rang, 2. Preis)
Wettbewerb Werkquartier, Ostermundigen (2. Rang)
Wettbewerb Schulanlage Utogrund, Zürich
Wettbewerb Verwaltungsbau, Liestal
Studienauftrag Kinder- und Jugendpsychiatrie (UPD), Bern (1. Rang)
Testplanung Arealentwicklung Bahnhof West, Münsingen
2024 Projektwettbewerb Siedlung Felsenrain, Zürich
Thesenkonkurrenz Campus Muristalden, Bern (4. Rang)
Studienauftrag Stammsiedlung Brunnenhof, Zürich (2. Rang)
Schulhaus Walka, Zermatt (offener Wettbewerb 2016, 1. Rang)
20 Denkmalgeschütztes Mehrfamilienhaus Hinterer Schermen 31, Ittigen

Laufende Projekte:
2025 21 Meinen Areal, Bern (Studienauftrag 2014, 1. Rang)
22 Kreuzstrasse 3–7, Zollikofen (Testplanung 2019, 1. Rang)
Vogtareal, Oberdiessbach (Testplanung 2018, 1. Rang)
Farbweg, Burgdorf (Studienauftrag 2018, 1. Rang)
Hirsbrunner Areal, Sumiswald
Wohnen im Park, Ittigen (Studienauftrag 2021, 1. Preis)
Taubenhalde 16, Bern (Wettbewerb 2020, 1. Rang)
Forschungs- und Ausbildungszentrum Universität, Bern (Wettbewerb 2020, 1. Rang)
Volksschule Weissenbühl, Bern (Wettbewerb 2022, 1. Rang)
Transformation Untermattweg 8, Bern
Wankdorffeldstrasse, Bern (Ideenstudie 2022, 1. Rang)
23 Zentrumszone Birrfeldstrasse, Mellingen (Wettbewerb 2025, 1. Rang)
Entwicklung Bell-Areal, Kriens (Studienauftrag 2021, 1. Rang)
Worblentalstrasse 68, Ittigen (Studienauftrag 2023, 1. Preis)
24 Wohnhochhaus Baufeld H, Lyss
Arealentwicklung Stutz, Lausen (Studienauftrag 2025, 1. Rang)

2

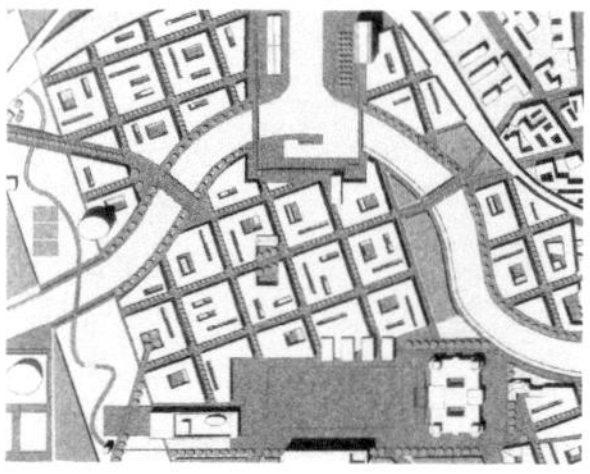
1

4

14

5

6

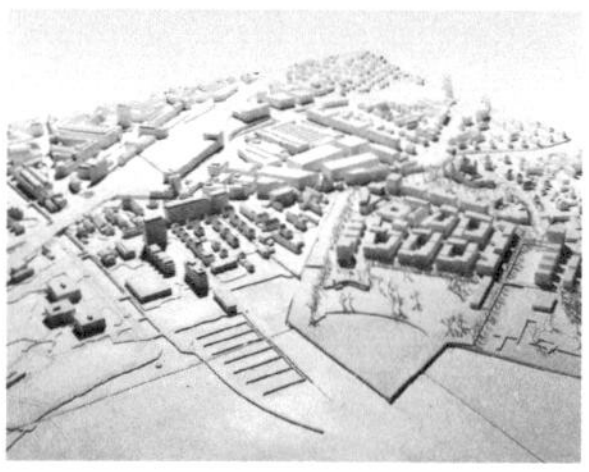
8

9

7

10

11

3

12

13

15

20

18

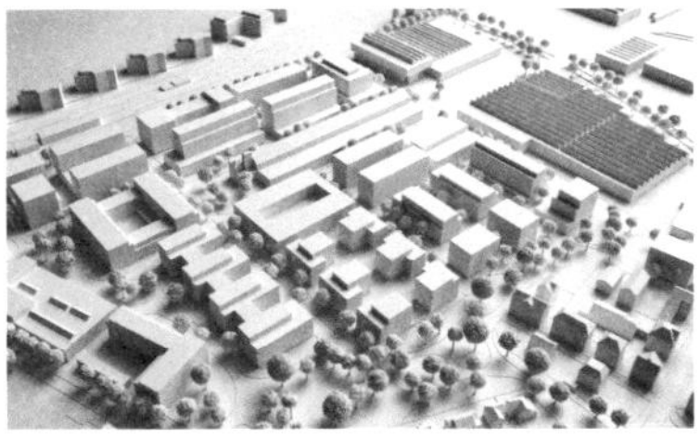

16

19

17

24

22

21

23

LIST OF WORKS

Selection of buildings, projects and competitions

1992	1	International competition, new Spreebogen government district, Berlin (3rd Prize)
1998	2	Office building, Ittigen (competition 1991, 1st Place)
2003	3	Synchrotron Lichtquelle, Villigen (study commission 1996, 1st Place)
2004	4	Master plan, Ban de Gasperich, Luxembourg
2006		Administrative building, Ittigen (competition 1997, 1st Place)
2007	5	Careum Campus, Zurich-Fluntern (competition 2000, 1st Place)
2010	6	International competition, master plan, Inselareal, Bern (2nd Place)
2011	7	Transformation, Alti Sagi, Innerberg
		Development strategy, University Hospital, Zurich
2013		Transformation, Gurtenbrauerei site, Wabern (site development 2004, design study / design commission 2008)
		Municipal development strategy, Rubigen
2014	8	Test planning, AggloLac, Biel (2nd Place)
		Listed apartment building, Gerberngasse, Bern
		Development strategy, Weiler, Ried
2015	9	Modernisation, Mobiliar office building, Bern
2016		Competition, complete renovation, Taubenhalde, Bern (1st Place)
2017	10	Apartment building, Lorrainestrasse, Bern
		Competition, Bubenberg railway station access, Bern
		Design commission, Marktgasse, Bern
		Test planning, centre development, Gümligen
2018		Design commission, van Baerle site, Münchenstein (1st Place)
		Competition, ZHAW campus, Winterthur (4th Place)
2019	11	Project development, dementia village, Wiedlisbach
		Competition, Viererfeld, Bern
		Competition, school campus, Sion
		Test planning, Gwattstrasse, Thun
		Contracted study, Du Lac residential building, Merligen
		Contracted study, Spühlirain, Schliern
	12	Test planning, Dreieck Süd, Zollikofen (1st Place)
		Competition, high-rise building, Lischenmoos, Gümligen (3rd Place)
	13	Competition, barracks site, Zurich (2nd Place / 1st Prize)
		Test planning, Fünf-Egg centre, Muri (1st Place)
2020	14	Wankdorf City II, Bern (competition 2015, 1st Place)
	15	Competition, Chirchbüel apartment buildings, Zumikon (1st Place)
		Competition, University Platztor Campus, St. Gallen (7th Place)
		Competition, Anderes Wohnen, Zollikofen
2021		Huebergass and district park, Bern (2017 competition, 1st Place)
		Competition, Building Site 04, University Hospital, Bern
	16	Test planning, Saurer Werk Zwei, Arbon (1st Place)
2022	17	Gangloff site, Bern
		Competition, Unterfeld Süd, Baar
2023		Anna Seiler House, Inselspital, Bern (competition 2014, 1st Place)
	18	Füllerichstrasse, Gümligen (competition 2018, 1st Place)
	19	Competition, cantonal school, Stein (3rd Place, 2nd Prize)
		Competition, Werkquartier, Ostermundigen (2nd Place)
		Competition, Utogrund School complex, Zurich
		Competition, administrative building, Liestal
		Contracted study, Child and Adolescent Psychiatry (UPD), Bern (1st Place)
		Test Planning, West Station area development, Münsingen
2024		Project competition, Felsenrain housing development, Zurich
		Competition for ideas, Muristalden campus, Bern (4th Place)
		Study commission, Brunnenhof housing estate, Zurich (2nd Place)
		Walka school building, Zermatt (open competition 2016, 1st Place)
	20	Listed apartment building, Hinterer Schermen 31, Ittigen
		Ongoing projects:
2025	21	Meinen Areal, Bern (contracted study 2014, 1st Place)
	22	Kreuzstrasse 3–7, Zollikofen (test planning 2019, 1st Place)
		Vogtareal, Oberdiessbach (test planning 2018, 1st Place)
		Farbweg, Burgdorf (contracted study 2018, 1st Place)
		Hirsbrunner Areal, Sumiswald
		Wohnen im Park, Ittigen (contracted study 2021, 1st Place)
		Taubenhalde 16, Bern (competition 2020, 1st Place)
		University research and training centre, Bern (competition 2020, 1st Place)
		Weissenbühl Primary School, Bern (competition 2022, 1st Place)
		Conversion, Untermattweg 8, Bern
		Wankdorffeldstrasse, Bern (ideas study 2022, 1st Place)
	23	Centre zone, Birrfeldstrasse, Mellingen (competition 2025, 1st Place)
		Development, Bell-Areal, Kriens (contracted study 2021, 1st Place)
		Worblentalstrasse 68, Ittigen (contracted study 2023, 1st Prize)
	24	Residential high-rise, Building Site H, Lyss
		Stutz area development, Lausen (contracted study 2025, 1st Place)

NICK GARTENMANN

1958	Geboren in Bern
1983–1986	Architekturstudium Eidgenössische Technische Hochschule ETH Zürich
1987–1988	Gerber Hungerbühler & Partner, Zürich
1987–	Übernahme Gartenmann Engineering AG
1989–	Gründung heutige GWJ Architektur (mit beiden Partner Mark Werren und Andreas Jöhri)
1992	Gründung Gartenmann & Partner Holding AG
1992–2012	Aufbau einer interdisziplinären Gruppe in den Gebieten Architektur, Generalplanung, Engineering sowie weiteren verwandten Bereichen mit insgesamt 500 Mitarbeitenden
2012–	Weiterführung der Gartenmann & Partner Holding AG und deren Tochtergesellschaften als Verwaltungsrat und Geschäftsführer

DONAT SENN

1966	Geboren in Bern
1983–1986	Lehre als Hochbauzeichner
1987–1990	Architekturstudium an der Ingenieurschule Burgdorf
1990–1992	Mitarbeit bei Matti Bürgi Ragaz Architekten, Bern
1992	Eintritt GWJ Architektur AG, Bern
1997–	Mitinhaber und Partner der GWJ Architektur AG, Bern und Zürich
2000	Aufnahme in den Schweizerischen Ingenieur- und Architektenverein (SIA) und REG A
2006–	Mitglied in Kommissionen für Ortsbild- und Gestaltungsfragen in Berner Gemeinden
2010–	Gründungsmitglied und Partner der AND Association
2014–2021	Professor für Architektur an der Berner Fachhochschule (BFH)

EVA HERREN

1978	Geboren in Chur
1996–1999	Lehre als Hochbauzeichnerin
2000–2004	Architekturstudium an der Zürcher Fachhochschule ZHAW Winterthur
2004–2015	Mitarbeit bei Romero Schaefle, Zürich, Nordisk Kombination Arkitekter, Stockholm, und Hildebrand Studios, Zürich
2014–2018	Lehrauftrag Berner Fachhochschule (BFH), Burgdorf
2016	Eintritt GWJ Architektur AG, Bern
2017	Aufnahme in den Schweizerischen Ingenieur- und Architektenverein (SIA)
2018–	Mitinhaberin und Partnerin der GWJ Architektur AG, Bern und Zürich

CHRISTIAN LASSER

1973	Geboren in Barcelona
1997–2001	Architekturstudium an der Escola Tècnica Superior d'Arquitectura (ETSAB), Barcelona
2000	Gründung MGV.LAB arquitectes, Barcelona
2001–2012	Mitinhaber und Partner von MGV.LAB arquitectes, Barcelona
2009–2012	Mitarbeit bei OAB, Barcelona, TdB Arquitectos, Barcelona, de Rham architectes, Lausanne, imaad rahmouni architects, Marrakech
2012	Eintritt GWJ Architektur AG, Bern
2018–	Mitinhaber und Partner der GWJ Architektur AG, Bern und Zürich

MAURIZIO CHIRICO

1978	Geboren in Bern
1995–1999	Lehre als Hochbauzeichner
2000–2004	Architekturstudium an der Berner Fachhochschule (BFH), Burgdorf
2004–2015	Mitarbeit bei Itten+Brechbühl AG, Bern, und Sollberger Bögli Architekten AG, Biel
2015	Eintritt GWJ Architektur AG, Bern
2021–	Associate der GWJ Architektur AG, Bern und Zürich
2022	Aufnahme in den Schweizerischen Ingenieur- und Architektenverein (SIA)

ANTONIA IMMENKAMP

1994	Geboren in Bern
2012–2015	Architekturstudium an der University of Applied Sciences, Frankfurt
2015–2016	Praktikum bei der GWJ Architektur AG, Bern
2016–2018	Architekturstudium an der Fachhochschule Nordwestschweiz (FHNW), Basel
2018	Eintritt GWJ Architektur AG, Bern
2024–	Associate der GWJ Architektur AG, Bern und Zürich

NICK GARTENMANN

1958	Born in Bern
1983–1986	Studied Architecture, ETH Zurich
1987–1988	Gerber Hungerbühler & Partner, Zurich
1987–	Takeover, Gartenmann Engineering AG
1989–	Founded today's GWJ Architecture (with Partners Mark Werren and Andreas Jöhri)
1992	Founded Gartenmann & Partner Holding AG
1992–2012	Development, interdisciplinary group in the fields of architecture, general planning, engineering and other related disciplines with a total of 500 employees
2012–	Continued management, Gartenmann & Partner Holding AG and its subsidiaries,

DONAT SENN

1966	Born in Bern
1983–1986	Apprenticeship as a structural draughtsman
1987–1990	Studied Architecture, Ingenieurschule Burgdorf
1990–1992	Employed, Matti Bürgi Ragaz Architekten, Bern
1992	Joined GWJ Architektur AG, Bern
1997–	Co-owner and Partner, GWJ Architektur AG, Bern and Zurich
2000	Member, Swiss Society of Engineers and Architects (SIA) and REG A
2006–	Member of commissions for townscape and design issues in Bernese municipalities
2010–	Founder member and Partner, AND Association
2014–2021	Professor of Architecture, Bern University of Applied Sciences (BFH)

EVA HERREN

1978	Born in Chur
1996–1999	Apprenticeship as a structural draughtswoman
2000–2004	Studied Architecture, ZHAW Winterthur
2004–2015	Employed, Romero Schaefle, Zurich, Nordisk Kombination Arkitekter, Stockholm and Hildebrand Studios, Zurich
2014–2018	Lecturer, Bern University of Applied Sciences (BFH), Burgdorf
2016	Joined GWJ Architektur AG, Bern
2017	Member, Swiss Society of Engineers and Architects (SIA)
2018–	Co-owner and Partner, GWJ Architektur AG, Bern and Zurich

CHRISTIAN LASSER

1973	Born in Barcelona
1997–2001	Studied Architecture, Escola Tècnica Superior d'Arquitectura (ETSAB), Barcelona
2000	Founded MGV.LAB arquitectes, Barcelona
2001–2012	Co-owner and Partner, MGV.LAB arquitectes, Barcelona
2009–2012	Collaborated with OAB, Barcelona, TdB Arquitectos, Barcelona, de Rham architectes, Lausanne, imaad rahmouni architects, Marrakech
2012	Joined GWJ Architektur AG, Bern
2018–	Co-owner and Partner, GWJ Architektur AG, Bern and Zurich

MAURIZIO CHIRICO

1978	Born in Bern
1995–1999	Apprenticeship as a structural draughtsman
2000–2004	Studied Architecture, Bern University of Applied Sciences (BFH), Burgdorf
2004–2015	Collaborated with Itten+Brechbühl AG, Bern and Sollberger Bögli Architekten AG, Biel
2015	Joined GWJ Architektur AG, Bern
2021–	Associate, GWJ Architektur AG, Bern and Zurich
2022	Member, Swiss Society of Engineers and Architects (SIA)

ANTONIA IMMENKAMP

1994	Born in Bern
2012–2015	Studied Architecture, University of Applied Sciences, Frankfurt
2015–2016	Internship, GWJ Architektur AG, Bern
2016–2018	Studied Architecture at the University of Applied Sciences and Arts Northwestern Switzerland (FHNW), Basel
2018	Joined GWJ Architektur AG, Bern
2024–	Associate, GWJ Architektur AG, Bern and Zurich

MITARBEITENDE

Aeschimann Lucas, Andres Nils, Andueza Aitor, Astudillo Valentina, Bögli Peter, Brügger Julien, Brühlmann Marilyn, Burkhardt Stefan, Carreira Filipe, Cebulla Marco, Czarnecka Marta, Deutsch Regula, Dridi Gioia, Durisch Sebastian, Egger Patrik, García Tania, Girardin Nicolas, Götz Robin, Gubler Bettina, Gugger Esther, Gurtner Theo, Hackiewicz Marcelina, Hadorn Jasmine, Hochhofer Stefan, Hofer Nicole, Hollenstein Claudio, Iseli Daniel, Januth Adrian, Kaszás Sándor, Kiew Selina, Lucy Leonie, Marro Barbara, Meyer Daniel, Müller Anna, Pecková Patrícia, Rentsch Mika, Richter Maxine, Sabo Meril, Schild Melvin, Schneider Céline, Schwander Tim, Scott Alejandra, Signer Stefan, Steiger Tanja, Uchenna Sabine, Walther Leander, Winkler Lukas, Wüthrich Christine, Zufferey Céline

EHEMALIGE MITARBEITENDE

Abt Peter, Aebi Margrit, Aebi Markus, Affolter Daniel, Al-Rafai-Lauter Sina, Andenmatten Timo, Assante Fabio, Assin Gabriel, Baciu Dan, Baumeister Anna, Benoit Gregory, Berger Thomas, Beutler Patric, Biermann Isabella, Blaser Simone, Bodmer Madeleine, Brügger Fabian, Buchmüller Pitt, Bunge Sophie, Burwitz Henning, Cardinale Marina, Caviezel-Ringli Marlene, Chatelet Christophe, Chaves Miguel, Cinkotsky Veronika, Cordes Dörthe, Däscher Sabine, De Simone Ivan, de Wurstemberger Nicolas, Demuth Marco, Dumont Lino, Ehrler Markus, Eigner Josephine, Elbe Christine, Erb Tobias, Erismann-Nielaba Anna, Fabbris Alberto, Fahl Karoline, Ferreira Junior, Flück Kaspar, Flück Ursi, Flühmann Rudenz, Forny Raphael, Freda Roberto, Friedl Anita, Gazzino Tiziano, Gerber Christoph, Giot Simon, Giovanelli Reto, Graf Sebastian, Grossniklaus Olivier, Grunder Adrian, Gubelmann Chris, Guggisberg Rahel, Haas Christina, Haftka Nina, Hähni Raphael, Haldemann Jonas, Handschick Cornelia, Härtner Dirk, Hasler Bernhard, Herzog Marcel, Heuer Christoph, Hinden Reto, Hirschi Ueli, Hofmeister Jacqueline, Hossepian Christ, Howald Matthias, Inäbnit Annina, Iseli Susanne, Izewska Zofia, Jäggi Natalie, Jean Aline, Jöhri Andreas, Jordi Roger, Kaderli Philipp, Känzig Ron, Käppeli Serge, Karatay Atilla, Kästli Pius, Kesselring Elias, Kilchenmann Lucy, Kilcher Nadine, Knobel Daniela, Knobloch Karim, Kohler Lia, Köhler-Roth Vilma, Kouvari Maria, Krummen-Aeschlimann Gabriela, Langenegger Marc, Lascheit Kamber Sabine, Lier Stefan, Löbner Claus, Loertscher McNally Simsa, Loukidou Eleni, Luginbühl Nicole, Lustenberger Philippe, Lüthi Simon, Lüthi Fabian, Mahmoudi Nordine, Malicki Sandra, Manchen Vanessa, Marquardt Ina, Marty Lorenz, Mävers Sebastian, Meyer Martin, Michailidou Natalia, Michel Fabian, Milos Daniel, Minnig Mandy, Misik Thomas, Mohr Lisa, Möller Christiane, Moser Simon, Müller Noé, Nef Julian, Neuenschwander Simon, Palomo Jan, Pellet-Strüby Monique, Pfeiffer Sabine, Pfenninger Annina, Pierrakou Chrysoula, Pscheor Michael, Pürro Maurin, Pyschny Thomas, Quattrocchi Fabio, Rauch Cati, Rautenberg Sandra, Reckermann Lili, Recrosio Peter, Reichen Philipp, Remund Patrick, Rochor Susann, Rohrer Fabienne, Roth Gregori, Rothe Alexander, Rüegger Mario, Russo Antonio, Sadek Arif, Schär Christine, Schär Michael, Scheidegger Ruedi, Scheurer Florian, Schihin Yves, Schmid Henrik, Schmidhalter Pascal, Schmidt Theres, Schneider Matthias, Schneider Stephan, Schneuwly Yvan, Schöbi Sandro, Schori Bernhard, Schulz Kerstin, Schwertfeger Christian, Sevinc Elena, Spänle Volker, Stalder Fabian, Steck Daniel, Steck Désirée, Steiner Jasmin, Steiner Sandra, Stettler Sacha, Stettler Jürg, Stettler Christian, Stössel Linda, Suchcicka Agata, Sutter Tanja, Szélpal Boris, Taraglio Elisa, Tejada Paloma, Teutsch Simon, Trabzon Serhan, Trapp Laurids, Tschumi Stefan, Tsetangtsang Topchen, Ulmi Nicole, Vacca Elisa, Varley Numa, Valeswaran Venston, Vidal-Breitenbach Renata, von Allmen Oliver, von Arx Lukas, Vranek Jakob, Wanger Yves, Wellner Maximilian, Werren Mark, Würsten Marc, Wüthrich Manuela, Wüthrich Sonja, Wyss Michael, Zahler Anna-Katharina, Zaugg Sabrina, Zen Ruffinen Xavier, Zimmerli Janine, Zimmermann Markus, Zuber Gerlinde, Zürcher Daniela

EMPLOYEES

Aeschimann Lucas, Andres Nils, Andueza Aitor, Astudillo Valentina, Bögli Peter, Brügger Julien, Brühlmann Marilyn, Burkhardt Stefan, Carreira Filipe, Cebulla Marco, Czarnecka Marta, Deutsch Regula, Dridi Gioia, Durisch Sebastian, Egger Patrik, García Tania, Girardin Nicolas, Götz Robin, Gubler Bettina, Gugger Esther, Gurtner Theo, Hackiewicz Marcelina, Hadorn Jasmine, Hochhofer Stefan, Hofer Nicole, Hollenstein Claudio, Iseli Daniel, Januth Adrian, Kaszás Sándor, Kiew Selina, Lucy Leonie, Marro Barbara, Meyer Daniel, Müller Anna, Pecková Patrícia, Rentsch Mika, Richter Maxine, Sabo Meril, Schild Melvin, Schneider Céline, Schwander Tim, Scott Alejandra, Signer Stefan, Steiger Tanja, Uchenna Sabine, Walther Leander, Winkler Lukas, Wüthrich Christine, Zufferey Céline

FORMER EMPLOYEES

Abt Peter, Aebi Margrit, Aebi Markus, Affolter Daniel, Al-Rafai-Lauter Sina, Andenmatten Timo, Assante Fabio, Assin Gabriel, Baciu Dan, Baumeister Anna, Benoit Gregory, Berger Thomas, Beutler Patric, Biermann Isabella, Blaser Simone, Bodmer Madeleine, Brügger Fabian, Buchmüller Pitt, Bunge Sophie, Burwitz Henning, Cardinale Marina, Caviezel-Ringli Marlene, Chatelet Christophe, Chaves Miguel, Cinkotsky Veronika, Cordes Dörthe, Däscher Sabine, De Simone Ivan, de Wurstemberger Nicolas, Demuth Marco, Dumont Lino, Ehrler Markus, Eigner Josephine, Elbe Christine, Erb Tobias, Erismann-Nielaba Anna, Fabbris Alberto, Fahl Karoline, Ferreira Junior, Flück Kaspar, Flück Ursi, Flühmann Rudenz, Forny Raphael, Freda Roberto, Friedl Anita, Gazzino Tiziano, Gerber Christoph, Giot Simon, Giovanelli Reto, Graf Sebastian, Grossniklaus Olivier, Grunder Adrian, Gubelmann Chris, Guggisberg Rahel, Haas Christina, Haftka Nina, Hähni Raphael, Haldemann Jonas, Handschick Cornelia, Härtner Dirk, Hasler Bernhard, Herzog Marcel, Heuer Christoph, Hinden Reto, Hirschi Ueli, Hofmeister Jacqueline, Hossepian Christ, Howald Matthias, Inäbnit Annina, Iseli Susanne, Izewska Zofia, Jäggi Natalie, Jean Aline, Jöhri Andreas, Jordi Roger, Kaderli Philipp, Känzig Ron, Käppeli Serge, Karatay Atilla, Kästli Pius, Kesselring Elias, Kilchenmann Lucy, Kilcher Nadine, Knobel Daniela, Knobloch Karim, Kohler Lia, Köhler-Roth Vilma, Kouvari Maria, Krummen-Aeschlimann Gabriela, Langenegger Marc, Lascheit Kamber Sabine, Lier Stefan, Löbner Claus, Loertscher McNally Simsa, Loukidou Eleni, Luginbühl Nicole, Lustenberger Philippe, Lüthi Simon, Lüthi Fabian, Mahmoudi Nordine, Malicki Sandra, Manchen Vanessa, Marquardt Ina, Marty Lorenz, Mävers Sebastian, Meyer Martin, Michailidou Natalia, Michel Fabian, Milos Daniel, Minnig Mandy, Misik Thomas, Mohr Lisa, Möller Christiane, Moser Simon, Müller Noé, Nef Julian, Neuenschwander Simon, Palomo Jan, Pellet-Strüby Monique, Pfeiffer Sabine, Pfenninger Annina, Pierrakou Chrysoula, Pscheor Michael, Pürro Maurin, Pyschny Thomas, Quattrocchi Fabio, Rauch Cati, Rautenberg Sandra, Reckermann Lili, Recrosio Peter, Reichen Philipp, Remund Patrick, Rochor Susann, Rohrer Fabienne, Roth Gregori, Rothe Alexander, Rüegger Mario, Russo Antonio, Sadek Arif, Schär Christine, Schär Michael, Scheidegger Ruedi, Scheurer Florian, Schihin Yves, Schmid Henrik, Schmidhalter Pascal, Schmidt Theres, Schneider Matthias, Schneider Stephan, Schneuwly Yvan, Schöbi Sandro, Schori Bernhard, Schulz Kerstin, Schwertfeger Christian, Sevinc Elena, Spänle Volker, Stalder Fabian, Steck Daniel, Steck Désirée, Steiner Jasmin, Steiner Sandra, Stettler Sacha, Stettler Jürg, Stettler Christian, Stössel Linda, Suchcicka Agata, Sutter Tanja, Szélpal Boris, Taraglio Elisa, Tejada Paloma, Teutsch Simon, Trabzon Serhan, Trapp Laurids, Tschumi Stefan, Tsetangtsang Topchen, Ulmi Nicole, Vacca Elisa, Varley Numa, Valeswaran Venston, Vidal-Breitenbach Renata, von Allmen Oliver, von Arx Lukas, Vranek Jakob, Wanger Yves, Wellner Maximilian, Werren Mark, Würsten Marc, Wüthrich Manuela, Wüthrich Sonja, Wyss Michael, Zahler Anna-Katharina, Zaugg Sabrina, Zen Ruffinen Xavier, Zimmerli Janine, Zimmermann Markus, Zuber Gerlinde, Zürcher Daniela

AUSSTELLUNGEN

2022	Schulhaus Walka, Zermatt, Le Concours Suisse. Une culture de l'architecture, Basel
2023	Huebergass, Bern, UIA World Congress of Architects, Kopenhagen
	Swiss Didac, Bern

AUSZEICHNUNGEN

2005	*Neue Horizonte Ideenpool holz 21 – Holzbaupreis 2005:* Verwaltungsgebäude Ittigen
2009	*Schweizer Holzbaupreis – Prix Lignum:* Verwaltungsgebäude Ittigen
2023	*Hase in Bronze für Landschaftsarchitektur:* Vorpark des Stadtteilparks Holligen, Huebergass, Bern
	Lean Construction Project Award: Anna-Seiler-Haus Inselspital, Bern
2024	*UIA 2030 Award* (Gewinner Kategorie 2): Huebergass, Bern
	Auszeichnung Berner Baukultur (Publikumspreis): Anna-Seiler-Haus Inselspital, Bern
	XAVER-Award (Silber): Anna-Seiler-Haus, Inselspital, Bern
2025	*best architects 2026:* Schulhaus Walka, Zermatt
	best architects 2026: Huebergass, Bern

BIBLIOGRAFIE

2009	Werner Huber (Hrsg.), *Bern baut. Ein Führer zur zeitgenössischen Architektur 1990–2010* [diverse Projekte], Zürich
2010	Roderick Hönig (Hrsg.), *Zürich wird gebaut. Ein Führer zur zeitgenössischen Architektur 1990–2010*, Zürich
2016	«Campus UVEK Ittigen», in: Bundesamt für Bauten und Logistik (Hrsg.): *Bundesbauten. Die Architektur der offiziellen Schweiz*, Zürich
2019	«Spuren suchen, Netze spannen, Räume formen» [Transformation Gurten Brauerei Areal, Wabern], in: *Hochparterre* (ca. 2019/20)
	Andres Herzog, «Architektur des Vergessens» [Demenzdorf Wiedlisbach], in: *Hochparterre*, Nr. 11, S. 36–39
	Paul Knüsel, «Gemeinnützig, aber effizienter» [Huebergass, Bern], in: *TEC21*, Nr. 50-51-52, S. 41–43
2020	Charles von Büren, «Baustein 07 im Inselareal Bern» [Forschungs- und Ausbildungszentrum Medizin, Universität Bern], in: *TEC21*, Nr. 9, S. 7–9
	«Absage an das Areal? Wettbewerb Gesamtinstandsetzung Kaserne Zürich», in: *Werk, Bauen + Wohnen*, Nr. 5, S. 44–47
	Philipp Jorisch, «Gläserne Krone und entblösste Struktur» [Wettbewerb Kasernenareal Zürich], in: *Hochparterre Wettbewerbe*, Nr. 2, S. 70–77
2021	«St. Galler Metamorphosen» [Wettbewerb Campus Platztor der Universität St. Gallen], in: *Hochparterre Wettbewerbe*, Nr. 4, S. 56
	Hubertus Adam, «Ein Stadtgarten für alle» [van Baerle Areal, Münchenstein], in: *Komplex 21*, Nr. 14, S. 164–171
2022	«Augen auf die Gasse» [Huebergass, Bern], in: *Werk, Bauen + Wohnen*, Nr. 12
	Marcel Bächtiger, «Die Schule ein Erlebnisraum» [Volksschule Goumoëns, Bern], in: *Hochparterre Wettbewerbe*, Nr. 2
	Charles von Büren, «Ein Holzpavillon für die Gumere-Matte» [Volksschule Goumoëns, Bern], in: *TEC21*, Nr. 12, S. 8–11
	«Campus UVEK Ittigen», in: *Bundesbauten*
2023	Paul Knüsel, «Eine Aneignung von Stadt mit Garten und Park» [Huebergass, Bern] in: *TEC21*, Nr. 40
	Gabriela Neuhaus, «Gemeinsam Park machen» [Huebergass, Stadtteilpark Holligen, Bern], in: *Hochparterre*, Nr. 12, S. 68–71
	Hubertus Adam, «Dem Leben eine Gasse» [Huebergass, Stadtteilpark Holligen, Bern], in: *Deutsche Bauzeitung*, Nr. 11, S. 12–18
	Natalie Schärer, «Die Insel setzt neue Standards» [Anna-Seiler-Haus, Bern], in: *TEC21*, Nr. 9
	Donat Senn, «Gurten Brauerei Areal: Bestehendes respektieren und Neues zulassen (zu Prozess 2)», in: Robert Braissant, *Zukunftsfähige Lebensräume. Grundlagen für urbane Transformation*, Basel, S. 185–188
	Michelle Schwarzenbach, «Im Dorf des Vergessens» [Demenzdorf Wiedlisbach], in: *Schweizer Illustrierte* 8, S. 46–50
2024	Markus Thome, «Historische Substanz als Herausforderung und Chance» [Denkmalgeschütztes Mehrfamilienhaus Hinterer Schermen, Ittigen], in: *Fachwerk Magazin* (Denkmalpflege Kanton Bern), S. 24–25
	Katharina Marchal, «Bauen unter alpinen Bedingungen» [Schulhaus Walka, Zermatt], in: *intelligent bauen*, Nr. 12, S. 24–27
	Noemi Grodtke, «Helles Holz zwischen dunklen Chalets» [Schulhaus Walka, Zermatt], in: *TEC21*, Nr. 28, S. 11–13
	«Weiterlernen» [Stadtteilpark Holligen, Bern], in: *Hochparterre*, Nr. 11, S. 62
	«Bildungsbauten. Walka, Zermatt», in: *Architektur + Technik*, Nr. 11, S. 6–13
	Gisela Graf, «Lernen unterm Matterhorn» [Schulhaus Walka, Zermatt], in: *Bauen modern*, Nr. 10, S. 26–31
	Cyrill Schmiedinger, «Ein neues Quartier für Bern» [Huebergass, Bern], in: *Architektur Aktuell*, Nr. 4, S. 78–87
	Achim Geissinger, «Anna-Seiler-Haus. Hauptgebäude des Inselspitals», in: *Deutsche Bauzeitung*, Nr. 4, S. 51
	Gisela Graf, «Im Herzen des Spitals» [Anna-Seiler-Haus, Inselspital, Bern], in: *Architektur + Technik*, Nr. 3, S. 12–15
	Claudia Moll, «Besser leben in Bern West» [Huebergass, Stadtteilpark Holligen, Bern], in: *Anthos Jahrbuch*, Nr. 4, S. 106–111
	[Huebergass, Bern], in: *Pro Bauhaus*, Nr. 12, S. 2–11
	«Pulsierende Siedlung» [Huebergass, Bern], in: *Architektur + Technik1*, Nr. 1, S. 10–15
	«Zentral in Zollikofen» [Kreuzstrasse 3–7, Zollikofen], in: *NZZ Real Estate Yearbook*, Edition 2023/24, S. 101
	Arno Heitland, «Neues Hauptgebäude mit energieeffizienten Fenstersystemen» [Anna-Seiler-Haus, Inselspital, Bern], in: *Fassade | Façade*, Nr. 1, S. 18–20
2025	«Lernen unterm Matterhorn. Bauen unter alpinen Bedingungen» [Schulhaus Walka, Zermatt], in: *Ernst & Sohn Special*, Nr. 3, S. 28–32
	«Madera de Barrio» [Huebergass, Bern], in: *Arquitectura Viva*, Nr. 2, S. 26–30
	GWJ Architektur, Reihe *De aedibus* Nr. 117, Luzern (Monografie, ISBN 978-3-03761-318-4)
	Tobias Schwarzer (Hrsg.), *best architects 26* [Huebergass, Bern; Schulhaus Walka, Zermatt], Monheim am Rhein

EXHIBITIONS

2022	Walka school building, Zermatt, Le Concours Suisse. Une culture de l'architecture, Basel
2023	Huebergass, Bern, UIA World Congress of Architects, Copenhagen
	Swiss Didac, Bern

AWARDS

2005	*Neue Horizonte Ideenpool holz 21 – Holzbaupreis 2005*: Administrative building, Ittigen
2009	*Schweizer Holzbaupreis – Prix Lignum:* Administrative building, Ittigen
2023	*Hase in Bronze für Landschaftsarchitektur:* Front section, Holligen district park, Huebergass, Bern
	Lean Construction Project Award: Anna-Seiler-Haus, Inselspital, Bern
2024	*UIA 2030 Award (Winner Category 2):* Huebergass, Bern
	Auszeichnung Berner Baukultur (Publicly Voted Prize): Anna-Seiler-Haus, Inselspital, Bern
	XAVER-Award (Silver): Anna-Seiler-Haus, Inselspital, Bern
2025	*best architects 2026:* Walka school building, Zermatt
	best architects 2026: Huebergass, Bern

BIBLIOGRAPHY

2009	Werner Huber (Ed.): *Bern baut. Ein Führer zur zeitgenössischen Architektur 1990–2010* [diverse Projekte], Zurich
2010	Roderick Hönig (Ed.): *Zürich wird gebaut. Ein Führer zur zeitgenössischen Architektur 1990–2010,* Zurich
2016	«Campus UVEK Ittigen». In: Bundesamt für Bauten und Logistik (Ed.): *Bundesbauten. Die Architektur der offiziellen Schweiz,* Zurich
2019	"Spuren suchen, Netze spannen, Räume formen" [Transformation, Gurten Brauerei Areal, Wabern]. In: *Hochparterre* (approx. 2019/20)
	Andres Herzog: "Architektur des Vergessens" [Wiedlisbach dementia village]. In: *Hochparterre,* No. 11, p. 36–39
	Paul Knüsel: "Gemeinnützig, aber effizienter" [Huebergass, Bern]. In: *TEC21*, Nos. 50-51-52, p. 41–43
2020	Charles von Büren: "Baustein 07 im Inselareal Bern" [Medical Research and Training Centre, University of Bern]. In: *TEC21,* No. 9, p. 7–9
	"Absage an das Areal? Wettbewerb Gesamtinstandsetzung Kaserne Zürich". In: *Werk, Bauen + Wohnen,* No. 5, p. 44–47
	Philipp Jorisch: "Gläserne Krone und entblösste Struktur" [competition, Kasernenareal Zurich]. In: *Hochparterre Wettbewerbe*, No. 2, p. 70–77
2021	"St. Galler Metamorphosen" [competition, Campus Platztor, University of St. Gallen]. In: *Hochparterre Wettbewerbe*, No. 4, p. 56
	Hubertus Adam: "Ein Stadtgarten für alle" [van Baerle Areal, Münchenstein]. In: *Komplex 21*, No. 14, p. 164–171
2022	"Augen auf die Gasse" [Huebergass, Bern]. In: *Werk, Bauen + Wohnen*, No. 12
	Marcel Bächtiger: "Die Schule ein Erlebnisraum" [Goumoëns Primary School, Bern]. In: *Hochparterre Wettbewerbe*, No. 2
	Charles von Büren: "Ein Holzpavillon für die Gumere-Matte" [Goumoëns Primary School, Bern]. In: *TEC21*, No. 12, p. 8–11
	"Campus UVEK Ittigen". In: *Bundesbauten*
2023	Paul Knüsel: "Eine Aneignung von Stadt mit Garten und Park" [Huebergass, Bern]. In: *TEC21*, No. 40
	Gabriela Neuhaus: "Gemeinsam Park machen" [Huebergass, Holligen district park, Bern]. In: *Hochparterre*, No. 12, p. 68–71
	Hubertus Adam: "Dem Leben eine Gasse" [Huebergass, Holligen district park, Bern]. In: *Deutsche Bauzeitung*, No. 11, p. 12–18
	Natalie Schärer: "Die Insel setzt neue Standards" [Anna-Seiler-Haus, Bern]. In: *TEC21*, No. 9
	Donat Senn: "Gurten Brauerei Areal: Bestehendes respektieren und Neues zulassen (zu Prozess 2)". In: Robert Braissant, *Zukunftsfähige Lebensräume. Grundlagen für urbane Transformation*, Basel, p. 185–188
	Michelle Schwarzenbach: "Im Dorf des Vergessens" [Wiedlisbach dementia village]. In: *Schweizer Illustrierte* 8, p. 46–50
2024	Markus Thome: "Historische Substanz als Herausforderung und Chance" [preservation-listed apartment building Hinterer Schermen, Ittigen]. In: *Fachwerk Magazin* (Denkmalpflege Kanton Bern), p. 24–25
	Katharina Marchal: "Bauen unter alpinen Bedingungen" [Walka school building, Zermatt]. In: *intelligent bauen* No. 12, p. 24–27
	Noemi Grodtke: "Helles Holz zwischen dunklen Chalets" [Walka school building, Zermatt]. In: *TEC21* No. 28, p. 11–13
	"Weiterlernen" [Holligen district park, Bern]. In: *Hochparterre* No. 11, p. 62
	"Bildungsbauten. Walka, Zermatt". In: *Architektur + Technik* No. 11, p. 6–13
	Gisela Graf: "Lernen unterm Matterhorn" [Walka school building, Zermatt]. In: *Bauen modern* No. 10, p. 26–31
	Cyrill Schmiedinger: "Ein neues Quartier für Bern" [Huebergass, Bern]. In: *Architektur Aktuell* No. 4, p. 78–87
	Achim Geissinger: "Anna-Seiler-Haus. Hauptgebäude des Inselspitals". In: *Deutsche Bauzeitung* No. 4, p. 51
	Gisela Graf: "Im Herzen des Spitals" [Anna-Seiler-Haus, Inselspital, Bern]. In: *Architektur + Technik*, No. 3, p. 12–15
	Claudia Moll: "Besser leben in Bern West" [Huebergass, Holligen district park, Bern]. In: *Anthos Jahrbuch* No. 4, p. 106–111
	[Huebergass, Bern]. In: *Pro Bauhaus* No. 12, p. 2–11
	"Pulsierende Siedlung" [Huebergass, Bern]. In: *Architektur + Technik* No. 1, p. 10–15
	"Zentral in Zollikofen" [Kreuzstrasse 3–7, Zollikofen]. In: *NZZ Real Estate Yearbook*, Edition 2023/24, p. 101
	Arno Heitland: "Neues Hauptgebäude mit energieeffizienten Fenstersystemen" [Anna-Seiler-Haus, Inselspital, Bern]. In: *Fassade | Façade* No. 1, p. 18–20
2025	"Lernen unterm Matterhorn. Bauen unter alpinen Bedingungen" [Walka school building, Zermatt]. In: *Ernst & Sohn Special* No. 3, p. 28–32
	"Madera de Barrio" [Huebergass, Bern]. In: *Arquitectura Viva* No. 2, p. 26–30
	GWJ Architektur, De aedibus series No. 117, Lucerne (monograph, ISBN 978-3-03761-318-4)
	Tobias Schwarzer (Ed.): *best architects 26* [Huebergass, Bern; Walka school building, Zermatt], Monheim am Rhein

AXEL SIMON
Einleitung

1966	Geboren in Düsseldorf
1983–1986	Lehre als Schriftsetzer
1989–1996	Architekturstudium an der Fachhochschule Düsseldorf und der HdK Berlin
1996–1999	Selbständige und angestellte Tätigkeit als Architekt in Berlin, Düsseldorf, Freiburg, Zürich
1998–2000	Nachdiplomstudium am Institut für Geschichte und Theorie der Architektur gta ETH, Zürich
2000–	Selbstständige Tätigkeit als Architekturkritiker
2007	Aufnahme als assoziiertes Mitglied des Bundes Schweizer Architektinnen und Architekten (BSA)
2010–	Redaktor der Zeitschrift Hochparterre, Zürich

SILKE SCHMEING
Projekttexte

1971	Geboren in Deutschland
1996–1999	Studium der Landschaftsarchitektur am ITR Rapperswil
1999–2007	Konzepterin und Texterin in Kommunikationsagenturen
2007–	Kommunikation und Fachjournalismus für die Planungsbranche in Anstellungen und selbständig

DANK

Wir danken für das Vertrauen – und manchmal auch die Geduld – der Bauherrinnen und Bauherren, die uns seit über 30 Jahren auf unserem Weg begleiten. Ohne sie wäre unsere Arbeit nicht das, was sie ist. Die direkte, enge Zusammenarbeit fordert und fördert unsere Kreativität auf ganz unterschiedliche Weise.

Wir danken für das Erprobte und Bewährte in der Zusammenarbeit mit Projektpartnern und Planerinnen. Ohne diese kooperative Basis wären unsere Lösungen nicht derart geschärft und robust. Darum schätzen wir die konstruktive Kooperation auf Augenhöhe in höchstem Masse.

Und wir danken für Unvergleichbarkeit: Nichts geht ohne wunderbare Mitarbeitende. Sie leisten täglich Grosses, setzen sich mit Engagement für die Bauherrinnen und Bauherren sowie für unsere Projekte ein. Und darüber hinaus – und das ist von unschätzbarem Wert – für das Miteinander. Nur so sind wir, was wir sind: GWJ .

AXEL SIMON
Introduction

1966	Born in Düsseldorf
1983–1986	Apprenticeship as a typesetter
1989–1996	Studied Architecture, University of Applied Sciences, Düsseldorf and the HdK Berlin
1996–1999	Freelance and employed work as an Architect in Berlin, Düsseldorf, Freiburg and Zurich
1998–2000	Postgraduate studies, Institute for the History and Theory of Architecture gta ETH, Zurich
2000–	Freelance work as an architecture critic
2007	Associate Member, Swiss Architects Association (BSA)
2010–	Editor, Hochparterre magazine, Zurich

SILKE SCHMEING
Project texts

1971	Born in Germany
1996–1999	Studied Landscape Architecture, ITR Rapperswil
1999–2007	Concept developer and copywriter for communications agencies
2007–	Communications and specialist journalist for the planning industry, freelance and employed positions

ACKNOWLEDGEMENTS

Thank you. For the trust – and sometimes the grace – of the clients who have accompanied our work for over 30 years. Without them, our oeuvre would not be what it is. Direct and close cooperation stimulates our creativity in many different ways.

Thank you. For tried and tested methods with project partners and planners. Without them, our solutions would not be so refined and robust. That is why we value constructive cooperation on an equal footing.

And: Thank you for the incomparability. Nothing works without great employees. You do incredible things every day, working hard for the clients and the projects. Furthermore – and this is immensely important – for ourselves, for each and every one of us, for our teamwork. It is the only way we can be what we are – we are GWJ.

FINANZIELLE UND IDEELLE UNTERSTÜTZUNG

Ein besonderer Dank gilt den Institutionen und Sponsorfirmen, deren finanzielle Unterstützungen wesentlich zum Entstehen dieser Buchreihe beitragen. Ihr kulturelles Engagement ermöglicht ein fruchtbares und freundschaftliches Zusammenwirken von Baukultur und Bauwirtschaft.

FINANCIAL AND CONCEPTUAL SUPPORT

Special thanks to our sponsors and institutions whose financial support has helped us so much with the production of this series of books. Their cultural commitment is a valuable contribution to fruitful and cordial collaboration between the culture and economics of architecture.

ZERMATT EINWOHNERGEMEINDE

schweizer kulturstiftung prohelvetia

SWISSLOS Kultur Kanton Bern

Burgergemeinde Bern

AMSTEIN + WALTHERT
Amstein + Walthert Bern AG

synaxis TRAGWERKSPLANUNG
solubois
zostera
Unternehmen der Synaxis-Gruppe

ORT
ORT AG für Landschaftsarchitektur, Zürich

GWJ Architektur
117. Band der Reihe *De aedibus*
Herausgegeben von: Heinz Wirz, Luzern
Konzept: Heinz Wirz; GWJ Architektur, Bern/Zürich
Textbeitrag: Axel Simon, Zürich
Objekttexte: Silke Schmeing, Oberengstringen
Textlektorat deutsch: Eva Guttmann, Graz
Übersetzung deutsch–englisch: Benjamin Liebelt, Berlin
Fotos: Mirjam Kluka, Zürich, S. 10–12; Tim Schwander, Bern, S. 13; map.bern.ch/geoportal: S. 14, 20 (oben), 24 (oben), 28 (oben), 34 (oben), 38 (oben), 42, 46, 60, 64, 68, 72; Thomas Haug, Zürich, S. 15–19; Roger Frei, Zürich, S. 21–23; Christoph Blank, Bern, S. 24 (unten); Alain Bucher, Bern, S. 28 (unten); A. Buser, Bern, S. 34 (unten); Bundesamt für Bauten und Logistik BBL, Bern, S. 38 (unten); Thomas Jantscher, Colombier, S. 43–45; www.google.ch: S. 50; Susanne Goldschmid, Bern, S. 51, 78, 83; geoportal.lu.ch: S. 56 (oben); Alexander Gempeler, Bern, S. 52–55; Franca Pedrazzetti, Luzern, S. 56 (unten); HGEsch Photography, Hennef, S. 73–75
Renderings: Play-Time, Barcelona, S. 25, 26, 29, 32/33, 35, 39, 47, 57, 58, 65, 69, 70
Redesign: BKVK, Basel – Beat Keusch, Angelina Köpplin-Stützle
Grafische Umsetzung: Quart Verlag Luzern
Lithos: Rica Egger, Printeria, Luzern
Druck: DZA Druckerei zu Altenburg GmbH

Der Quart Verlag wird vom Bundesamt für Kultur für die Jahre 2021–2025 unterstützt.

ISBN 978-3-03761-318-4

GWJ Architektur
Volume 117 of the series *De aedibus*
Edited by: Heinz Wirz, Lucerne
Concept: Heinz Wirz; GWJ Architektur, Bern/Zurich
Article: Axel Simon, Zurich
Project descriptions: Silke Schmeing, Oberengstringen
German text editing: Eva Guttmann, Graz
German–English translation: Benjamin Liebelt, Berlin
Photos: Mirjam Kluka, Zurich, p. 10–12; Tim Schwander, Bern, p. 13; map.bern.ch/geoportal: p. 14, 20 (top), 24 (top), 28 (top), 34 (top), 38 (top), 42, 46, 60, 64, 68, 72; Thomas Haug, Zurich, p. 15–19; Roger Frei, Zurich, p. 21–23; Christoph Blank, Bern, p. 24 (bottom); Alain Bucher, Bern, p. 28 (bottom); A. Buser, Bern, p. 34 (bottom); Bundesamt für Bauten und Logistik BBL, Bern, p. 38 (bottom); Thomas Jantscher, Colombier, p. 43–45; www.google.ch: p. 50; Susanne Goldschmid, Bern, p. 51, 78, 83; geoportal.lu.ch: p. 56 (top); Alexander Gempeler, Bern, p. 52–55; Franca Pedrazzetti, Lucerne, p. 56 (bottom); HGEsch Photography, Hennef, p. 73–75
Renderings: Play-Time, Barcelona, p. 25, 26, 29, 32/33, 35, 39, 47, 57, 58, 65, 69, 70
Redesign: BKVK, Basel – Beat Keusch, Angelina Köpplin-Stützle
Graphic design: Quart Verlag Luzern
Lithos: Rica Egger, Printeria, Lucerne
Printing: DZA Druckerei zu Altenburg GmbH

Quart Publishers is being supported by the Federal Office of Culture for the years 2021–2025.

ISBN 978-3-03761-318-4

Produktsicherheit / Product safety
Verantwortliche Person gemäss EU-Verordnung / Responsible person pursuant to EU Regulation 2023/988 (GPSR):
GVA Gemeinsame Verlagsauslieferung Göttingen GmbH & Co. KG
Postfach / Post Box 2021
37010 Göttingen
Deutschland / Germany
T +49 551 384 200 0
info@gva-verlage.de

Quart Verlag GmbH
Denkmalstrasse 2, CH-6006 Luzern
books@quart.ch, T +41 41 420 20 82, www.quart.ch

De aedibus
Zeitgenössische Architekturschaffende und ihre Bauten

De aedibus
Contemporary architects and their buildings

117 GWJ Architektur (de/en)
116 Gäumann Lüdi von der Ropp (de/en)
115 Lütolf und Scheuner (de/en)
114 Renato Maurizio Architekten (de/en)
113 Oxid Architektur (de/en)
112 dl-a, designlab-architecture (de/en, fr/en)
111 LVPH (de/en, fr)
110 CLR architectes (de/en, fr/en)
109 Brandenberger Kloter (de/en)
108 Menzi Bürgler Kuithan (de/en)
107 Frei Architekten (de/en)
106 Darlington Meier (de/en)
105 Sollberger Bögli (de/en)
104 Gus Wüstemann (de/en)
103 frey architectes (de/en)
102 Masswerk Architekten (de/en)
101 Giorgis Rodriguez (de/en, es/fr)
100 Carlos Martinez (de/en)
99 Stocker Lee (de/en, it)
98 Roman Hutter (de/en)
97 Bachelard Wagner (de/en, fr)
96 Alain Wolff architectes (de/en, fr)
95 Horisberger Wagen (de/en)
94 Pont12 (de/en, fr)
93 Christian Dupraz (de/en, fr)
92 group8 (de/en, fr/en)
91 MPH (de/en, fr/en)
90 Spillmann Echsle (de/en)
89 Andy Senn (de/en)
88 Architetti Tibiletti Associati (de/en)
87 Zach + Zünd (de/en)
86 Kistler Vogt (de/en)
85 Sylla Widmann (de/en, fr/en)
84 Aebi & Vincent Architekten (de/en)
83 Baumberger & Stegmeier (de/en)
82 L-architectes (de/en, de/fr)
81 Frei Rezakhanlou (de/en)
80 weberbrunner (de/en)
79 Meyer Piattini (de/en)
78 meier + associés architectes (de/en, de/fr)
77 Lin Robbe Seiler (de/en, de/fr)
76 Meier Leder (de/en)
75 Butikofer de Oliveira Vernay (de/en)
74 Elisabeth & Martin Boesch (de/en)
73 spaceshop Architekten (de/en)
72 Kast Kaeppeli (de/en)
71 Philippe Meyer (de/en, fr)
70 bartbuchhofer (de/en)
69 Hauenstein La Roche Schedler (de/en)
68 Graeme Mann & Patricia Capua Mann (de/en)
67 Esposito Javet (de/en, de/fr)
66 Galletti Matter (de/en, de/fr)
65 Fruehauf, Henry & Viladoms (de/en)
64 Jakob Steib (de/en)
63 bunq (de/en)
62 Jean-Paul Jaccaud (de/en, de/fr)
61 huggenbergerfries (de/en)
60 Berrel Berrel Kräutler (de/en)
59 Pierre-Alain Dupraz (de/en, de/fr)
58 Cometti Truffer (de/en)
57 Joos & Mathys (de/en)
56 Lacroix Chessex (de/en)
55 Savioz Fabrizzi (de/en, de/fr)
54 Boegli Kramp (de/en)
53 Zita Cotti (de/en)
52 Oestreich + Schmid (de/en)
51 Stump & Schibli Architekten (de/en)
50 Luca Gazzaniga (de/en)
49 Guignard & Saner (de/en)
48 Morger + Dettli (de/en)
47 Charles Pictet (de/en)
46 Armando Ruinelli + Partner (de/en/it)
45 Luca Selva Architekten (de/en)
44 Luca Deon (de/en)
43 2b (de/en)
42 Durisch + Nolli (de/en)
41 sabarchitekten (de/en)
40 Beat Rothen (de/en)
39 Atelier Bonnet (de/en)
38 Novaron (de/en)
37 Althammer Hochuli (de/en)
36 Schneider & Schneider (de/en)
35 Frei & Ehrensperger (de, en)
34 Liechti Graf Zumsteg (de/en)
33 Adrian Streich (de/en)
32 Daniele Marques (de/en)
31 Neff Neumann (de/en)
30 Giraudi Wettstein (de/en)
29 Steinmann & Schmid (de/en)
28 Matthias Ackermann (de/en)
27 Aeby & Perneger (de/en)
26 Bakker & Blanc (de/en)
25 Markus Wespi Jérôme de Meuron (de/en)
24 Bauart (de/en, de/fr)
23 Knapkiewicz & Fickert (de/en)
22 Marcel Ferrier (de/en)
21 Wild Bär Architekten (de/en)
20 Enzmann + Fischer (de/en)
19 Mierta und Kurt Lazzarini (de/en)
18 Rolf Mühlethaler (de/en)
17 Pablo Horváth (de/en)
16 Brauen + Wälchli (de/en)
15 E2A Eckert Eckert Architekten (de/en)
14 Lussi + Halter (de/en)
13 Philipp Brühwiler (de/en)
12 Scheitlin – Syfrig + Partner (de/en)
11 Vittorio Magnago Lampugnani (de/en)
10 Bonnard Woeffray (de/en, de/fr)
9 Graber Pulver (de/en)
8 Burkhalter Sumi / Makiol Wiederkehr (de/en)
7 Gigon/Guyer (de, en)
6 Andrea Bassi (de, fr, en)
5 Dieter Jüngling und Andreas Hagmann (de, en)
4 Beat Consoni (de, en)
3 Max Bosshard & Christoph Luchsinger (de)
2 Miroslav Šik (de, en, it)
1 Valentin Bearth & Andrea Deplazes (de, en, it)

books@quart.ch, www.quart.ch